Rethink Yourself

Rethink Yourself

Change Your Thinking (Not Yourself)
to Build Your Self-Esteem

Zach Leezer, LCSW

Rethink Yourself
Change Your Thinking (Not Yourself) to Build Your Self-Esteem
Zach Leezer, LCSW

Structural editing by Laura Bontje, Laura Bontje Editing Services
Copyediting by Erika Steeves, E.S. Editing Services
Cover design by J.R. Caines
Interior design and images by Jason Craft, Crafticity LLC

Although I am a therapist, I am not your therapist. Reading this book does not create a therapist–client relationship between us. This book should not be used as a substitute for the advice of a competent therapist authorized to practice in your jurisdiction and familiar with your situation.

Please note that I don't make any guarantees about the results of the information applied in this book. Your ultimate success or failure will be the result of your own efforts, your particular situation, and many other circumstances beyond my knowledge and control.

First U.S. Edition, 2024

Print ISBN: 979-8-218-31608-2
Ebook ISBN: 979-8-218-55485-9

Printed in the U.S.A.

Contents

Chapter 1

A Good Investment

Take a moment to think about who you are. What kinds of things come to mind? Are they positive, negative, neutral, or a combination of the three? If you have low self-esteem, maybe your mind jumped right to your imperfections, inadequacies, and mistakes. Maybe you thought of a few things you like about yourself but immediately questioned if they're good enough. Or maybe you're not even really sure who you are or what you bring to the table. What if instead you thought of yourself the same way you think of someone you admire and respect? You might be thinking, *I'd have to change a lot about myself for that to ever happen*. Well, this book isn't going to help you with that. That's because self-esteem has nothing to do with who you are and everything to do with who you *think* you are. You don't need to change anything about yourself as a person to build your self-esteem; you *do* need to change your mind about yourself, though.

As a psychotherapist, I've made self-esteem my primary specialization because I recognize that self-esteem has an enormous impact on our mental health and overall well-being. Nathaniel Branden, a pioneering expert on self-esteem, described it as "the immune system of consciousness,"[1] which highlights exactly why it's so important. Our immune system's job is to protect us from bacteria, viruses, toxins, and other threats. Even though our immune system isn't perfect and can't guarantee we won't be harmed by these threats, it does a pretty good job at making us more resilient to them. And if we become infected with a virus, our immune system helps us fight it off and return to health.

Our self-esteem functions in a similar way, except the threats aren't viruses and germs. They're anxiety, depression, stress, and other types of mental and emotional distress. Our self-esteem helps to protect us from these things, even if it's not completely bulletproof.

Of course, even though our immune system helps fight off illness, that doesn't mean we never need medical care; similarly, our self-esteem helps us face challenges with confidence, but sometimes we need a little more support than self-esteem alone can offer. Nevertheless, self-esteem plays an important role in helping our minds function properly, and building your self-esteem will surely boost your mind's immune system.

How to Read This Book

This book demands engagement. Simply reading this book without practicing what you learn won't get you very far; you'll only see results if you engage with the content. Each chapter ends with a self-compassion exercise designed to help you practice the concepts and approaches covered in the chapter. Think about them as opportunities to change the way you think about yourself, bit by bit.

Unlike with that mystery novel you just can't put down, I'll actually encourage you to put this book down several times. This is to ensure you take the time to really immerse yourself in the content. Simply imagining yourself completing the self-compassion exercises without actually putting the techniques you learn into practice won't give you the outcome you're looking for. Nothing you'll read in this book will make you like yourself—it's what you *do* with what's in this book that will make the difference.

You may feel excited about the prospect of having a stronger self-esteem and want to rush through the content as quickly as you can, but I encourage you to take your time. This isn't a race to the finish line. Self-esteem can't be rushed anyway; your thoughts about yourself are deep-rooted and won't change quickly. Why rush through the book if your self-esteem can't be rushed? This is the start of a lifelong process of fostering a healthy self-image, not a mission with a finite objective.

Key Terms

Before you start with the hands-on work, let's lay some groundwork by defining a few key terms I refer to throughout this book: *self-concept, self-esteem, self-worth*, and *self-compassion*. At first, this might seem like a frivolous attempt to split hairs. You might want to skip ahead, but I urge you not to. These terms are interconnected and often get confused for each other. So let's make sure we're on the same page about what these concepts mean.

Believe it or not, psychologists and therapists can't seem to come to a consensus on the definition of *self-esteem*. Definitions vary slightly from source to source. Self-esteem experts have their own slightly unique definition, which shapes their approach to understanding and building it. For you to get the most out of this book (or any book on self-esteem), it's important to understand the nuances between these related concepts.

Self-Concept

Your self-concept is simply your perception of yourself: a description, not an evaluation. It's the answer to the question "Who am I?" For example, a piece of your self-concept might be that you're funny and that you have a procrastination habit. It includes both your strengths and your struggles, but it doesn't get into how you *feel* about these factors. Your self-esteem is where your opinion comes in. Think of your self-concept like a mirror. Instead of reflecting your physical appearance, your self-concept reflects your mind's image of who you are. It represents your awareness of all your personal qualities. If the reflection is fair and realistic, then your self-concept tends to be accurate.

A harsh and relentless inner critic can warp your perception of yourself, reflecting back a distorted and unappealing image, like a fun-house mirror. It minimizes your strengths and allows them to be overshadowed by your limitations. Instead of thinking of yourself as funny, you might think of yourself as *kind of funny, but not as funny as your best friend*, or you might even downplay that characteristic so much that you overlook it entirely. And instead of thinking of yourself as having a procrastination habit, you might think of yourself as *incompetent, lazy,* or *totally incapable of getting anything done*.

As you can see, your self-concept is subjective. It's not a reflection of who you are, just who you *think* you are. That means you might not see yourself exactly the same way your friends, family, or coworkers see you. Often the reason people struggle with their self-esteem is because their self-concept is warped. With the right tools, you can modify how you perceive yourself without changing a single thing about who you are as a person. My hope is that after finishing this book, your self-concept will look a lot different than it does now, even though you will have stayed exactly the same.

Self-Concept:

- Your subjective description of yourself
- Value-neutral (not "good" or "bad")

Self-Esteem

Self-esteem is your personal opinion of yourself, usually determined by how good, likable, and capable you think you are. Unlike your self-concept, your self-esteem is a value judgment. It's your interpretation of your self-concept. This book will help you rethink that interpretation, but it won't change your self-esteem on its own. Addressing self-esteem directly would be like me trying to convince you to *like* the warped reflection you see when you look in the mirror. That will never happen!

What this book can do is help you flatten that mirror so that you can assess your goodness, likability, and capability based on what's really there—not based on the self-criticisms that distort your perception of yourself. It's easier to evaluate yourself when your self-concept is fair and realistic. A flat mirror allows you to see your weaknesses and limitations for what they are. It's not about ignoring your weaknesses in favor of your strengths or constructing an illusion of perfection. In fact, people with healthy self-esteem generally have no problem acknowledging their shortcomings—because they're not threatened by them.

A seemingly intuitive approach to improving your self-esteem is to improve *yourself*. You might think that refining your strengths and overcoming your weaknesses will make you like yourself more. People take this approach quite often, but they usually don't get the results they were hoping for. That's because self-improvement doesn't change the thought patterns that caused you to develop low self-esteem in the first place. If you try to change yourself without flattening your fun-house mirror first (your warped self-concept), you'll struggle to approve of the still-distorted image you continue to see. That's why the primary goal of this book is to help you flatten your fun-house mirror so you can see yourself as you are.

> I know, simply changing the mirror and nothing else isn't a guarantee you'll end up liking yourself. After all, what if you still don't like what you see after you've flattened the mirror? I'll address that in chapter 11, which is about accepting yourself in spite of your limitations. Regardless of the possibility that flattening your mirror won't be quite enough, it has to at least be part of the process. Personal growth won't lead to improved self-esteem when the methods you use to evaluate yourself are unfair. You need to work on that part first, and that's exactly what this book will teach you how to do.

To build your self-esteem, you need to learn how to acknowledge your limitations without allowing them to threaten you. If this sounds impossible, I'm willing to bet you already do it in some regard. Think about your best friend. You love and value them, and you see them in a positive way. Although you're aware of their weaknesses, and you've witnessed them make some (or several) mistakes, you don't let those things overshadow any of their positive qualities. They're still your friend who you hold in high regard, despite their imperfections. This is what self-esteem looks like. It's not about seeing yourself as faultless; it's about taking stock of all factors fairly, seeing yourself for who you are, and being satisfied instead of overly judgmental.

Self-Esteem:

- Your subjective interpretation of your self-concept (how it makes you feel)
- Your perception of how good, likable, and capable you are

Self-Worth

Your self-worth represents your ability to recognize and honor your innate human value. Your worth is innate and inalienable; it exists whether you can see it right now or not. Therefore, your self-worth isn't a measure of *how worthy you think you are* but whether you're willing to *accept* your innate worth as it is.

A common myth about self-worth is that you can improve it the same way you improve your self-esteem—by changing the way you think about yourself. Instead, it's about recognizing that you're worthy simply because you exist, not because of who you are or what you've done. You don't have to be special to be worthy. You don't have to earn your worth either. Your worth is tied to your humanity. It exists because you exist. Even with a warped fun-house mirror, you can (and should) still recognize that the image reflected back at you is a human being. And that human being has innate value.

Self-worth isn't the same as self-importance. You can't compare your innate worth to someone else's. Don't be afraid that recognizing your worth will make you self-centered or arrogant. If you can recognize that your own worth is innate and unearned, then you can recognize the same for others.

Self-esteem and *self-worth* are often used interchangeably, but it's important to understand how they're different. Self-esteem is based on hundreds of ever-changing factors, while self-worth is based on only one thing: your connection to your innate worth (and your innate worth doesn't change). The problem with using *self-esteem* and *self-worth* interchangeably is that it gives mistakes and self-criticism the power to make you feel worthless. And when you feel unworthy, it's hard to grant yourself the compassion you need because you question whether you even deserve it.

Self-Worth:

- Your ability to recognize your innate human value
- Can't be earned, only accepted

Self-Compassion

As the name suggests, *self-compassion* refers to both acts and feelings of compassion toward yourself. When you're self-compassionate, you are fair, gentle, kind, and understanding toward yourself, *even after you've failed at something*. Sometimes self-compassion gets misrepresented or is portrayed in ways that turn a lot of people off. For that reason, let's be clear about what self-compassion is *not*.

Self-compassion is NOT the opposite of self-discipline.

Self-compassion is NOT a "get-out-of-jail-free card" when you've done something wrong.

Self-compassion is NOT selfish entitlement.

Self-compassion is NOT disregarding the needs and feelings of others.

Self-compassion is NOT mushy-gushy feelings of self-love.

Self-compassion is NOT just for spiritual people.

This book will help you harmonize self-compassion with self-discipline, accountability, humility, and respect for others. These are not mutually exclusive concepts.

Self-compassion has to be built on a foundation of unconditional self-worth. This book will encourage you to be kinder to yourself, but you have to believe that you deserve that kindness first. You *will not* and *cannot* give yourself any more compassion than you think you deserve. Any attempt at self-compassion will feel empty if it doesn't feel deserved. Building genuine self-esteem involves extending self-compassion, and to do that, you have to believe you're worthy of that compassion. That's where we'll start.

Self-Compassion

- How you treat yourself
- Has to feel "deserved" in order to be genuine

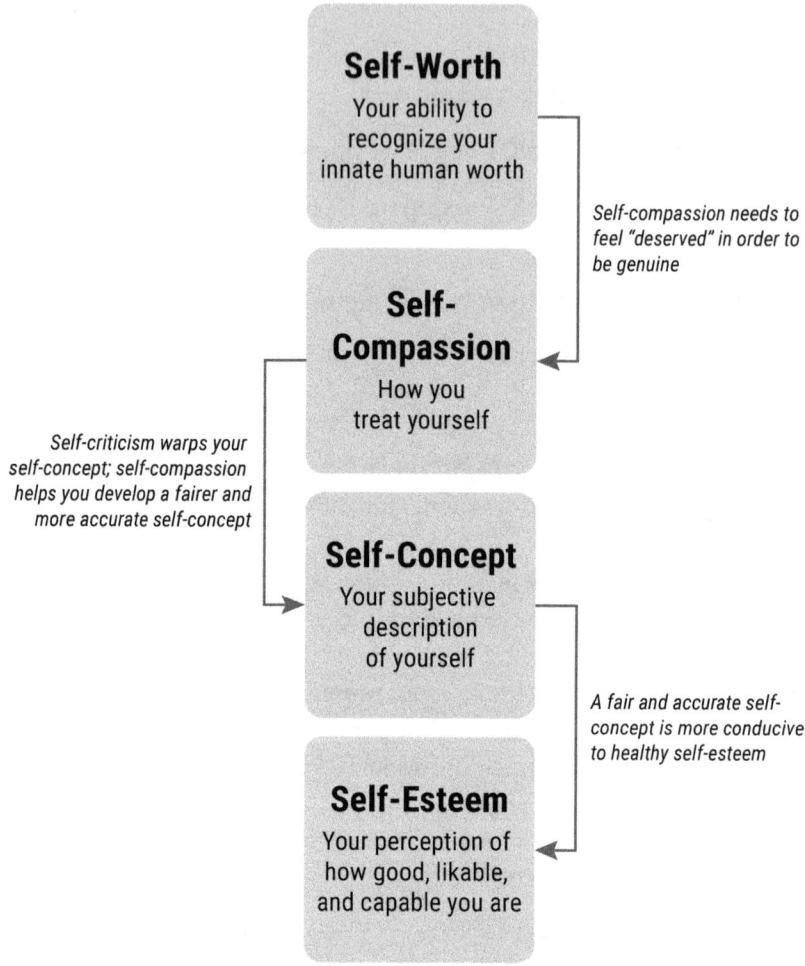

Self-Worth
Your ability to recognize your innate human worth

Self-compassion needs to feel "deserved" in order to be genuine

Self-Compassion
How you treat yourself

Self-criticism warps your self-concept; self-compassion helps you develop a fairer and more accurate self-concept

Self-Concept
Your subjective description of yourself

A fair and accurate self-concept is more conducive to healthy self-esteem

Self-Esteem
Your perception of how good, likable, and capable you are

Why Is Self-Worth So Important?

Even though this book is primarily about building a strong self-esteem, it's impossible to do that if we don't include self-worth in the process. Without unconditional self-worth, you won't believe you deserve the self-compassion it takes to flatten your fun-house mirror. There's just no other way to go about it.

Aside from unconditional self-worth being a necessary step in the process of building your self-esteem, self-worth is a crucial element of overall well-being. To understand the difference self-worth can make in your life, compare your life with and without it. First, think about what your life would be like if you could accept your innate worth without objection. You'd believe that you deserve happiness, so you'd freely seek out things that make you happy. When you're disrespected, you'd never doubt that you deserve better, so you'd reject the mistreatment. You wouldn't be afraid to accept love because you'd know you're worthy of it. Your connection to your innate human value would make your life meaningful and joyful.

Now think about what your life would be like if you denied your innate worth every chance you got. You would think of yourself as completely and totally valueless. Without a shred of self-worth, you'd have no motivation to seek out the things that add value to your life. You wouldn't pursue happiness, respect, or love because you wouldn't believe you're worthy of them. You'd only pursue what you think you deserve (which isn't much).

Simply put, you just can't thrive without self-worth—it's a cornerstone of psychological well-being. In fact, low self-worth is a core feature of depression,[2] and research shows that a strong sense of self-worth can enhance a person's ability to cope with stress and hardship.[3] When you recognize your innate worth, you're able to approach life's challenges with less fear of failure, rejection, or shame. So if you want to work on your self-esteem, you can't ignore your self-worth. In fact, that's exactly where you need to start.

You're Worth Investing In

You're probably reading this book because your self-esteem is low and you want to change that. You want to learn how to see yourself in a more positive light and stop criticizing yourself so much. Sounds great, right? A common misconception about building self-esteem is that it's a feel-good process. Of course, parts of it do feel really good. But there are undoubtedly parts that will challenge you and even make you feel uncomfortable. That's because what building your self-esteem really boils down to is change, and change is hard. Keep in mind, the goal isn't to change *you* but to change how you *think* about yourself. Regardless, mental change is still change, and it's still challenging.

Take a minute to think about why you chose to spend your time and money on this book. Your answer is probably something along the lines of "I want to feel better about myself." But consider what that means. Improving your self-esteem will require some precious resources—time, energy, effort, and perseverance. I refer to them as investments. Now, I'm a therapist, not an investment banker, so I know next to nothing about investing. But what I do know is that nobody ever invests in anything they see no value in. That would be a foolish investment! So why did you choose to invest your time and money in this book? Could it be that you've decided (probably subconsciously) that you're worth investing in?

I hope you can recognize that the act of reading this book is evidence that something deep inside you recognizes your innate worth. How does that realization make you feel? Many of my clients have described it like a punch in the gut. It may feel like a hard-hitting place to begin, but there's a reason for that. Before you start working on rethinking yourself, you need to break down a paradox that's easy to get trapped in. It's the idea that you have to earn your self-worth through some sort of defining trait or accomplishment.

"If I just lost 15 pounds, I'd feel more worthy."

"If I got a promotion, I'd feel more worthy."

"If I had more friends, I'd feel more worthy."

These are statements I hear all the time. When someone expresses a sentiment like these, it's usually because they don't buy the idea that their worth is innate and inalienable. But there are a few fundamental problems that arise from attempting to earn your self-worth. The first and most obvious problem is that these kinds of statements place conditions on your innate human value. They give your changing circumstances the power to make you feel worthless. And basing your human value on dynamic factors like your weight, salary, or popularity is profoundly unfair. It subjects your self-worth to never-ending volatility, which is detrimental to your well-being. It also reinforces the belief that you're not a whole person until you find some sort of missing piece to fill.

But there's an even bigger problem here. Aside from being completely demoralizing, believing you have to earn your worth is also a trap. First of all, personal change requires effort. And it's really difficult to put effort into such an endeavor if you don't believe you're worth the effort. Making that change will be next to impossible without a sense of innate worth to give you reason to pursue it.

There are only two possible outcomes to this approach:

- You'll never be able to make the change you think you need to earn your self-worth, and as a result, you'll internalize a sense of failure that will sink you deeper into worthlessness.

- Even if you're somehow able to achieve that change, you won't allow yourself to accept it as "good enough," because you never felt deserving of it in the first place.

Either way, you won't end up finding what you were looking for. Self-worth will elude you every single time you try to earn it. The only way to "find" your self-worth is to recognize that your innate worth already exists, no matter where you are in life.

At first, the notion that human worth is innate and universal might seem to go against everything you were taught. But thinking of human worth as something you can measure and compare comes with a lot of baggage. Many of the worst atrocities in history occurred because one group of people thought they were more innately valuable than another group of people. And thinking of yourself as less valuable than those around you is incredibly self-destructive. It's dangerous and frankly impossible to calculate something as complex as a human being's value. Instead, the only sensible approach to self-worth is to recognize that your worth already exists, no matter where you are in life.

It may take some time, but it's important that you separate your innate human value from your individual attributes. Your value cannot be measured by your wealth, popularity, ability, appearance, or any other factor. So before you start the work of building your self-esteem, you need to accept this statement: "I'm worth investing in." You wouldn't be reading this book if you didn't already at least partially believe it.

"I'm worth investing in."

If you're not able to say this statement with at least a little conviction, don't continue just yet. Give it a day or two to work itself out in your brain, then come back. You don't need to say it into a mirror, and you don't need to conjure up any warm, fuzzy feelings. The statement just needs to make sense to you logically. If you want to improve your self-esteem, you must be willing to invest in yourself, and you won't do that if you don't think you're worth the investment. Before you move on to the hard work ahead, you need to believe there's a reason for it.

The most logical reason is simply that *you're worth investing in*.

Now let's get started.

Chapter 2

Your Self-Worth Is Right in Front of You

If you want to improve your self-esteem, you'll need to make an investment in yourself. And in order to make that investment, you need to believe that you're worth the effort. That's why self-worth has to be the foundation that self-esteem is built on. But finding your self-worth doesn't have to be a fluffy "just love yourself" process. More realistically, it's about working through the ways your thoughts obstruct you from seeing your innate value.

Low self-worth can manifest in several ways. The most obvious is when we tell ourselves that we're worthless. But sometimes it's more subtle than that. Sometimes it's when we try to measure our value by how successful, thin, popular, or exceptional we are. Sometimes it's when we deprioritize our needs because we don't think they really matter. No matter how low self-worth manifests in your life, it's important that you establish an unconditional sense of self-worth as the first step in building your self-esteem.

As you recall, your self-worth is simply whether or not you believe you're worthy. And your worth is derived solely from the fact that you exist. You don't need to make yourself worthy, because you already are. You just need to train yourself to see what's already there. In some ways you already do, whether you realize it or not. The fact that you decided to read this book is evidence that something inside you believes that you're worth making an effort for. And when you start to look for more evidence like that, you'll eventually realize that your innate worth is a reality that's hard to deny.

How to Find Your Self-Worth

Finding your self-worth involves three main steps, which we'll work through in detail throughout the chapter.

The first step is knowing your worth.

This means understanding what you're worthy *of*. And that's determined by your humanity, not your accomplishments. No matter how warped your mirror (a.k.a. your self-concept) is, you have to acknowledge that what you're looking at in that mirror is a human being. And as a human being, you have innate value, whether you're able to recognize that right now or not.

The second step is honoring your worth.

Once you know your worth, you have to act like it. This step is important because knowing your worth is incomplete on its own. Think of it this way: if you value someone else, does that value only exist in your head, or is it also evident in your actions? Seeing someone as innately valuable is both an attitude and a practice. If you value someone, you typically demonstrate that through your actions. In the same way, if you value yourself, then your actions would naturally reflect that.

The third step is the most crucial: seeing your worth.

This involves recognizing your efforts to honor your worth in step 2. No matter how much you show someone you value them, they will only feel valued if they notice your efforts. The same goes for you. If you don't acknowledge your own efforts, it's easy to ignore your innate worth or question whether it even exists. Let's go through these in detail.

Step 1: Knowing Your Worth

You can't find your self-worth if you don't know what you're looking for. You need to understand what you're worthy *of*. Don't forget—your worth isn't measured by your talents and accomplishments, but instead by your humanity.

By virtue of simply existing as a human being, you have a set of basic needs. Now, there's room for discussion on exactly what these needs are since there's no natural law to reference. We can all agree that humans have basic physiological needs like food, water, and shelter. Those needs nurture our survival, but there's a lot more to our humanity than just surviving. We also have needs of a higher order. And you, like everyone else, are worthy of having these needs met *right now*. Not after you've made some self-improvements. *Now*.

So what are these needs anyway? They're all the intangible stuff that collectively make up the human experience. I call them "intrinsic human needs." Survival needs alone are not enough; intrinsic needs are what give our lives meaning. Think of survival needs as the walls and roof that make up a house and intrinsic needs as the personal touches that make it a home.

Below is a list I developed of 15 intrinsic human needs. This list is not a declaration but rather a suggestion to get you started thinking about what you're worthy of. Please review this list with an open mind.

Intrinsic Human Needs

Appreciation: You are worthy of acknowledgment, approval, and admiration for your unique characteristics and perspectives.

Comfort: You are worthy of having your reasonable preferences honored and existing in a physical and social environment that is pleasant and peaceful.

Compassion: You are worthy of empathy, validation, and kindness—even, and especially, in difficult circumstances.

Fairness: You are worthy of being held to reasonable standards and expectations that account for your capabilities, limitations, and resources without exaggeration or misrepresentation.

Forgiveness: You are worthy of opportunities to correct your mistakes without bearing their burden for an unfair amount of time.

Growth: You are worthy of experiencing progress and mastery in matters that align with your values and abilities.

Happiness: You are worthy of contentment, life satisfaction, and overall well-being.

Health: You are worthy of having your physical, emotional, spiritual, relational, financial, intellectual, and environmental needs met.

Help: You are worthy of having your needs recognized and met without the expectation of reciprocation.

Respect: You are worthy of being regarded by others and yourself in a way that honors your humanity.

Love/Companionship: You are worthy of genuine mutual trust, commitment, and endearment, regardless of the amount of love you feel for yourself.

Patience: You are worthy of the grace to be imperfect, and to be shown tolerance in times of frustration.

Rest: You are worthy of allowing your body and mind to be in serenity whenever needed, without the requirement to earn it through productivity.

Safety: You are worthy of an adequate level of stability and predictability in your life, free from worry of physical and emotional harm.

Self-Determination: You are worthy of the freedom to make decisions about your own life and circumstances, as long as these decisions don't subject others to undue harm.

As you read this list, you may have felt some resistance to a few of the items. That's okay. You don't have to agree with all of them, and your beliefs might not align perfectly with mine. Feel free to add other needs, or even remove or rephrase any you disagree with. However, please consider each need carefully before you make modifications. Just because you experience resistance to a new idea doesn't necessarily mean it's wrong. Before you modify any of these items, let's address some common sticking points to make sure any pushback you feel isn't because of misunderstanding.

Worthy, Not Guaranteed

Simply being worthy of each of these intrinsic needs doesn't mean they're owed to you or you're guaranteed to get them 100% of the time. Intrinsic needs are more nuanced than that. For example, you're worthy of love from *someone*, but not anyone you want it from. In other words, nobody is obligated to love you. So if a person decides that they don't want to give you love (romantic or platonic), that doesn't mean you're not worthy of love; it just means that person doesn't want to fulfill that need. This idea applies to all your intrinsic needs. Nobody is under any obligation to fulfill any of your intrinsic needs, but it's your responsibility to do whatever you can to pursue them.

Even though it's your job to pursue your intrinsic needs, self-worth is not a license to shirk responsibilities and expectations to pursue selfish goals. It doesn't liberate you from your responsibility to be a good person or a good friend. For example, even though you're worthy of comfort, you may sometimes decide to do things that are uncomfortable for the sake of people you care about. Compromising on your own needs from time to time isn't a violation of your innate worth, as long as you don't make it a habit. It's up to you to decide how your intrinsic needs relate to those around you and what you consider fair and reasonable. Most of the time, your own intrinsic needs won't impact anyone else, but occasionally, you'll encounter conflicting interests. In those situations, you'll need to decide what's best for yourself and others.

Pursued, Not Earned

There might be certain items on the list of intrinsic needs that go against what you were taught. You may have been told that things like growth, rest, and forgiveness have to be earned. Here are some common examples:

> Only exceptionally hardworking people can achieve growth.
>
> You can't rest until you've been productive enough to deserve it.
>
> Some wrongs just can't be forgiven.

If you're feeling some pushback to any of these intrinsic needs, it may be because you believe they shouldn't be given freely. That part is true. You can't expect any intrinsic needs to just fall into your lap; it's your responsibility to pursue them. But that's not the same as earning them.

Remember, you have to believe that you're worthy of something in order to make the necessary investments to pursue it. If you start with the assumption that you're not worthy of growth, you'll find it very difficult to ever motivate yourself to put in the necessary work to grow. You need to believe you're worthy of it for it to eventually happen, or at least to fully accept it when it does happen. Of course this involves effort, but self-worth should be an ingredient of that effort, not a product of it.

When you feel worthy of something, you put in the necessary work to make it happen. Not the other way around.

Step 2: Honoring Your Worth

Now that you know what you're worthy of, it's important that you honor that worth too. Remember, knowledge of your innate worth isn't enough on its own. If that knowledge isn't reflected in your actions, it doesn't mean much. The only way to honor your worth is by making an effort to meet your intrinsic needs. After all, if your worth is tied to your humanity, then honoring your worth just means honoring your basic human needs.

All of us deserve to have our basic needs met, no matter our personal qualities. You don't have to like yourself in order to honor your worth. Liking yourself and seeing your value are two very different things, and it's dangerous to get them mixed up. Just because you don't like something doesn't make it worthless or undeserving. The same goes for you. You may not like yourself (yet), but no matter how warped and distorted your self-concept is, you can and should still recognize your humanity.

Your self-worth is reflected in your everyday actions (for better or worse). With rock-bottom self-worth, you deny your intrinsic needs every chance you get. After all, if you don't matter, then your needs aren't important enough to honor. But knowing your innate worth allows you to pursue your needs. And any time your actions honor your innate worth, I call that an "act of self-worth."

Acts of self-worth are tangible representations of your self-worth. They include any self-beneficial effort you make to pursue, honor, or reinforce any of your intrinsic needs. Engaging in acts of self-worth means conducting yourself in a way that honors your humanity. You simply cannot honor your own humanity while depriving yourself of your intrinsic human needs. Acts of self-worth are merely gestures that demonstrate to yourself that you matter enough to have your needs met.

These acts can be big or small. The big ones are what I refer to as investments. Reading this book to work on your self-esteem is one example of an investment. You're putting in a lot of time and effort to pursue your need for self-esteem (which I would categorize under your need for appreciation or even happiness). But more often, acts of self-worth are everyday things we don't give much thought to, like staying hydrated (health), spending time with loved ones (love/connection), wearing a seatbelt (safety), or setting aside time to relax (rest).

Engaging in acts of self-worth doesn't always need to involve intentional effort, though. Sometimes they can simply be attitudes or reactions. For example, if you feel frustrated or hurt after being disrespected, your emotional reaction is an act of self-worth because it stems from your recognition that you deserve better than the disrespect you received. Mentally rejecting criticism from a hypercritical family member can also be an act of self-worth. Even though it's not a concrete action, you're still honoring and protecting your intrinsic needs, even if only internally.

You might have noticed that the bar is pretty low for what counts as an act of self-worth. They're very rarely transformative on their own. If you're used to thinking that your self-worth needs to be earned, then the idea that all you really have to do is meet your basic needs can feel insufficient. Usually when I introduce the concept of acts of self-worth to my clients, they remark, "But I already do most of those things," to which I make sure to reply, "Yes, and that's why noticing them is so important." But more on that step later in the chapter.

There's a direct cause-and-effect relationship between self-worth and acts of self-worth. But make no mistake, self-worth isn't the effect, it's the cause. In other words, acts of self-worth don't *make* you worthy. Instead, they *honor* the innate worth that's already there. It's easy to get it mixed up, but doing that can be damaging to your self-worth. Remember, no action can dictate your worth.

Now, you may not do everything perfectly, and you may miss some important opportunities to engage in acts of self-worth, but that's okay. Perfection isn't the goal because "perfectly worthy" isn't a real thing. You might feel that you don't do "enough" to keep yourself happy or safe or comfortable. You'll likely do better at those things once you've finished this book. All that really matters right now is that you do *something* to honor your worth in your day-to-day life, even if your efforts aren't always successful. Some intrinsic needs are certainly harder to satisfy than others.

Step 3: Seeing Your Worth

Here's the most important part of the process. You have to acknowledge your acts of self-worth in order for them to mean anything to you. No amount of honoring your worth is going to make you feel worthy unless you notice those efforts. Think of it this way: if you make an effort to show your loved ones that you value them, but they don't notice, they're not going to feel valued. And the same is true for you.

You might think that finding your self-worth just involves doing more acts of self-worth. There's certainly value in that approach, but more realistically, it means recognizing the acts of self-worth that you're already doing. The problem isn't that you don't do them; it's that you don't notice when you do. You may have trouble thinking of yourself as someone who matters, but many of your actions say otherwise (like reading this book, for example). You just need to train yourself to see that.

This final step encourages you to spot your acts of self-worth when you do them. That doesn't mean you have to exaggerate or brag about them. You just need to understand what your acts of self-worth imply—that your needs matter because you matter.

When you're getting started, it can be hard to know if something counts as an act of self-worth or if it's meaningful enough to even credit. Usually, acts of self-worth are small and easy to miss, so if you're ever unsure, ask yourself this question:

"If I weren't worthy of _____ , why would I _____ ?"

This question makes your self-worth pretty hard to deny. If you were completely worthless, you'd have no reason to do anything for your own benefit (even really small things). But since you *do* do these things, you can recognize that something deep inside you knows that you're worth it. Why else would you do any acts of self-worth?

We are hardwired to care for our needs, so we pursue many of our intrinsic needs naturally. Sure, we could all probably improve on a few (or all) of them. But generally speaking, when we look hard enough, it's not hard to find evidence of the ways we already care for those needs. The important part here is recognizing the times we already do this.

Seeing Your Worth[lessness]?

Seeing your worth can be difficult when there also seem to be glaring signs that you're worthless. After all, internalized feelings of worthlessness don't come from nowhere. Usually they stem from observations that seem to point to the conclusion that you don't matter. You don't need to ignore those signs or lie to yourself; however, you *should* question whether they're actually signs or just misperceptions.

A common reason someone might believe they're worthless is because they feel they've committed some sort of unforgivable offense in the past. But that's not very good "evidence" of worthlessness. By now you know that your actions don't dictate your worth. And if actions can't make you worthy, then the inverse must also be true: no action can make you *unworthy*. Past regrets may obstruct you from seeing your innate worth, but they certainly don't have the power to alienate you from it. If you struggle with feelings of regret, chapter 7 on addressing the harsh inner critic will be helpful. For now, just remember that no mistake is powerful enough to make you worthless.

You should also be careful not to let the actions of other people dictate your worth. Something I hear a lot is "People treat me like trash all the time, so it must mean that I am trash." But this logic has several flaws.

First, how others decide to treat you isn't a fair way to assess your innate value. Unfortunately, good and worthy people are treated badly all the time. That doesn't mean they're not good and worthy. It just means that others don't treat them with the respect and compassion they deserve. Remember, nobody is obligated to show you respect and compassion, even though it would be nice if they did.

Second, it's possible other people don't honor your innate worth because they don't see it. After all, you might not see your own worth yet, so it's possible for other people to miss it too. Just because someone else disregards your innate worth doesn't mean it doesn't exist.

Finally, it's highly unlikely that everyone in your life treats you poorly. There are probably plenty of people who do give you the respect and compassion you deserve. When you assume you're worthless because certain people treat you like you are, you're probably unfairly magnifying the importance of the negative treatment you receive and minimizing the importance of the positive treatment. That's not proof that you're worthless; it's a thinking error that points you to an inaccurate and unfair conclusion.

Self-Compassion Exercise:

Noticing Your Acts of Self-Worth

The practice of noticing is key. That's what this self-compassion exercise asks you to do. Remember, acts of self-worth can be mundane and seemingly insignificant; they don't need to be transformative or extraordinary. If you're ever unsure whether something counts as an act of self-worth, ask yourself this question:

"If I weren't worthy of _____ , why would I _____ ?"

In the spaces on the next page, jot down the acts of self-worth you notice yourself doing. It's important to use the phrasing "I am worthy of _____ , so I _____ ." This eliminates any risk of misunderstanding self-worth as the product of your acts of self-worth rather than the motivation for those acts. Be as specific as possible in your examples, and take all the time you need. In fact, don't rush this. It's something you should work on over time, not all at once. This exercise isn't meant to be *completed* but instead *engaged with*. You'll never be "done" recognizing your acts of self-worth, just like you'll never be "done" learning or growing or making healthy choices. It's a process, not a destination. I've provided 30 spaces, but don't feel compelled to stop at 30 acts of self-worth if you're able to keep going.

On the other hand, if 30 sounds like a daunting amount, think of it as a challenge. Try to come up with enough acts of self-worth to fill all 30 spaces (that's just two acts per intrinsic need!). Don't move on to the next chapter until you've filled all 30 spaces. For your reference, I've included the same list from earlier in the chapter, as well as a few examples of acts of self-worth.

To download a free copy of this worksheet, visit rethinkyourself.info/worksheets or scan the QR code in the back of the book.

Appreciation: You are worthy of acknowledgment, approval, and admiration for your unique characteristics and perspectives.

Example: *I am worthy of appreciation, so I surround myself with people who value me.*

I am worthy of appreciation, so I

_____.

I am worthy of appreciation, so I

_____.

Comfort: You are worthy of having your reasonable preferences honored, and to exist in a physical and social environment that is pleasant and peaceful.

Example: *I am worthy of comfort, so I choose comfortable clothing.*

I am worthy of comfort, so I

_____.

I am worthy of comfort, so I

_____.

Compassion: You are worthy of empathy, validation, and kindness, even and especially in difficult circumstances.

Example: *I am worthy of compassion, so I call my best friend when I need a pep talk.*

I am worthy of compassion, so I

_____.

I am worthy of compassion, so I

_____.

Fairness: You are worthy of being held to reasonable standards and expectations that account for your capabilities, limitations, and resources, without exaggeration or misrepresentation.

Example: *I am worthy of fairness, so I advocate for myself at work to protect me from unfair treatment.*

I am worthy of fairness, so I

_____.

I am worthy of fairness, so I

_____.

Forgiveness: You are worthy of opportunities to correct your mistakes without bearing their burden for an unfair amount of time.

Example: *I am worthy of forgiveness, so I apologize when I do something wrong.*

I am worthy of forgiveness, so I

_____.

I am worthy of forgiveness, so I

_____.

Growth: You are worthy of experiencing progress and mastery in matters that align with your values and abilities.

Example: *I am worthy of growth, so I set short- and long-term goals for myself.*

I am worthy of growth, so I

_____.

I am worthy of growth, so I

_____.

Happiness: You are worthy of contentment, life satisfaction, and overall well-being.

Example: *I am worthy of happiness, so I set aside time to do things I enjoy.*

I am worthy of happiness, so I

_____.

I am worthy of happiness, so I

_____.

Health: You are worthy of having your physical, emotional, spiritual, relational, financial, intellectual, and environmental needs met.

Example: *I am worthy of health, so I brush and floss my teeth every day.*

I am worthy of health, so I

_____.

I am worthy of health, so I

_____.

Help: You are worthy of having your needs recognized and met without the expectation of reciprocation.

Example: *I am worthy of help, so I rely on my partner to do tasks I'm not good at.*

I am worthy of help, so I

_____.

I am worthy of help, so I

_____.

Respect: You are worthy of being regarded by others and yourself in a way that honors your humanity.

Example: *I am worthy of respect, so I ignore disrespectful comments from customers at work.*

I am worthy of respect, so I

_____.

I am worthy of respect, so I

_____.

Love/Companionship: You are worthy of genuine mutual trust, commitment, and endearment, regardless of the amount of love you feel for yourself.

Example: *I am worthy of love/companionship, so I go on dates, even though they make me anxious.*

I am worthy of love/companionship, so I

_____.

I am worthy of love/companionship, so I

_____.

Patience: You are worthy of the grace to be imperfect and to be shown tolerance in times of frustration.

Example: *I am worthy of patience, so I feel frustrated when someone is short with me.*

I am worthy of patience, so I

_____.

I am worthy of patience, so I

_____.

Rest: You are worthy of allowing your body and mind to be in serenity whenever needed, without the requirement to earn it through productivity.

Example: *I am worthy of rest, so I sleep in on the weekends.*

I am worthy of rest, so I

_____.

I am worthy of rest, so I

_____.

Safety: You are worthy of an adequate level of stability and predictability in your life, free from worry of physical and emotional harm.

Example: *I am worthy of safety, so I keep the doors and windows to my home locked.*

I am worthy of safety, so I

_____.

I am worthy of safety, so I

_____.

Self-determination: You are worthy of the freedom to make decisions about your own life and circumstances, as long as these decisions don't subject others to undue harm.

Example: *I am worthy of self-determination, so I form my own opinions instead of following what others think.*

I am worthy of self-determination, so I

_____.

I am worthy of self-determination, so I

_____.

Self-Respect:
The Crucial First Step to a Strong Self-Esteem

Okay, so you are actually worthy, and I hope by this point you believe that to some extent. Not only is your self-worth the foundation that you'll build your self-esteem on, but it's also your first line of defense against your inner critic. Every time it hurls insults at you, it's violating your intrinsic need for respect and failing to honor the fact that you deserve better. But now that you've found your self-worth, you're not going to let that keep happening, right?

We usually think of respect in the context of interpersonal situations only. We see it as something we give to and receive from others, but we don't always think about whether we're giving respect to ourselves. Consider all the ways you might disrespect yourself: calling yourself names, deeming yourself worthless, or being relentlessly self-critical. If someone else did those things to you, you'd feel completely disrespected, maybe even offended. So why do you do them to yourself?

It's funny how little thought we give to our own internal monologues. A thought pops up, and more times than not, we just kind of go with it. If we think, *I'm a lazy slob*, we might take that as truth and proceed through the rest of our day as if we were in fact a lazy slob. We don't often take a thought like that and think, *Wow, that was mean. Did I deserve that?* On the other hand, if someone said those exact words to us, we'd probably recognize the words as unkind and disrespectful—*even if we agree with them*.

Don't get mad at yourself for *having* self-criticism, though. It's your response to your self-criticism that really matters. Unwanted thoughts such as self-criticism are incredibly normal. If they weren't, nobody would have thoughts that scare, frustrate, surprise, or demean them. When an unwanted self-critical thought pops into your head, use this response:

"That was disrespectful, and I deserve respect."

Throughout this book, you'll learn more targeted approaches to tame your inner critic. But until then, just start with this one. From now on, respond to all your <u>harsh</u> self-criticisms with the statement above. I underlined the word "harsh" because it's important here. Only use this approach in response to harsh self-talk. Sometimes self-criticism is totally reasonable, even if it doesn't feel good. I call that "legitimate self-criticism." For example, negative thoughts that hold us accountable, such as *I shouldn't have lied to my best friend like that* or *I really need to reach out to my mom more*, aren't harsh, even though they're also not positive. Harsh criticism I'm referring to here are thoughts like *I'm a trash can of a person* or *I can't do anything right*. These are criticisms that are excessive or mean-spirited.

Feel free to put your own spin on this statement: "That was disrespectful, and I deserve respect." There are endless ways you can call attention to your worthiness of respect, so choose wording that feels genuine and meaningful to you. Here are some suggestions to get you started:

> "That was mean, and I deserve kindness."
>
> "I deserve to be treated better."
>
> "I wouldn't disrespect my friend like that, so I shouldn't disrespect myself like that."

Even if you agree with your harsh self-criticism, you can still recognize that it's disrespectful. And don't worry just yet about proving your harsh self-criticism wrong. Evaluating the truthfulness of self-criticism is a big undertaking, so we'll get to it later. For now, just focus on the disrespect, even if your harsh self-criticism seems true. Just because something is "true" doesn't mean it should be said (or thought).

Chapter 3

Your Inner Critic Is Not All Yours

Your inner critic is a big part of why your self-esteem is low. It shatters your confidence, makes you doubt yourself, and relentlessly fixates on your flaws. It just won't seem to leave you alone. You've probably tried to think more positively, but that approach doesn't always work. To change the way you think about yourself, you first need to understand how your thought patterns developed. Then you can approach your self-criticism more effectively. This chapter will help you do that.

Understanding Your Inner Critic

In order to take control of your inner critic, you have to understand it first. If you don't know how it operates, you can't disarm it. To get a better understanding of how your inner critic works, you need to know three main principles:

1. Almost everyone has an inner critic

I say "almost" because there may be some exceptions, like in cases of narcissism and psychopathy, but these are extremely rare. Most people think of their inner critic as their enemy, but one of the positive things it does for us is promote growth and accountability. It helps us evaluate ourselves and bring awareness to the things we can improve on. Imagine how difficult personal growth would be if you couldn't think critically about yourself. When our inner critic functions the way it's meant to, it guides our growth and keeps us accountable. This is what I call "legitimate self-criticism." You'll learn more about the purpose of your inner critic in chapter 8, but for now, just know that there's nothing wrong with you for having an inner critic. The problem isn't that you have one—it's that your inner critic is too harsh.

2. Dysfunction of your inner critic doesn't happen on its own

The reason your inner critic is so harsh is because it was influenced by outside factors that interfere with the way you think about yourself. Certain forces throughout your life may have invaded your inner critic, co-opted its normal functions, and caused it to work against you instead of for you.

Common outside forces that invade the inner critic:

- Bullying
- Parents/Caregivers
- Unhealthy or Abusive Relationships
- Media
- Gender Norms
- Discrimination/Inequality
- Mental Illness (Stigma)
- Trauma
- Capitalism
- Individualistic Values

We'll explore these in more detail later in the chapter.

Your brain isn't meant to work against you. At some point an outside force acted against you, and your brain simply adapted. Maybe you can already pinpoint what that outside force was. Even if you can't do that right now, this chapter will help you figure it out.

When your inner critic has been co-opted by an outside force, it uses blame, insults, and judgment. It no longer guides growth and accountability the way it's meant to; instead, it does the exact opposite. It can leave you feeling so broken that you wonder if you're even capable of growth at all. A harsh inner critic completely warps your fun-house mirror.

3. Your inner critic can't heal until you untangle it from the outside force that interfered with it

It's important to understand how outside forces affect your inner critic. You can't take back control of your inner critic if you're not sure where your inner critic ends and the outside force begins. That's what we'll explore in this chapter.

Initially it might seem far-fetched that at some point we can lose control over our inner critic to some outside force. After all, we have free will and should take responsibility for our problems . . . right? The truth is, we're social creatures. And as social creatures, we're easily influenced by the people around us, our culture, and even social systems. We really can't separate ourselves from our environment. It has an immeasurable impact on who we are and what we think.

To be clear, taking control of your self-criticism doesn't just mean taking the blame off yourself and projecting it onto something else. Blame isn't a helpful solution for anything. Instead of looking for who or what to blame, focus instead on developing a solid understanding of the impact these outside forces have had on you. Once you've developed a solid understanding of what influenced your thinking, you'll learn a technique that will help you take back some control.

Critical Outside Forces

When I talk with my clients about their negative self-talk, I'm always curious where it comes from. There's something unnatural about self-hate. It isn't inborn; more often it's ingrained, and we need to figure out where it started. Usually there's a moment where it clicks, and they'll say, "Oh my god, that's exactly what my ex-boyfriend used to say to me" or "I never realized it, but I got told that all the time after I was diagnosed with ADHD." Nobody is born with these self-destructive thoughts. Even though they may sound like your voice, most likely they started out as someone else's voice and then slowly started to sound like yours.

Your first task in this chapter is to identify the outside force(s) that has taken over your inner critic. To help you do that, we'll explore the most common culprits and how they could diminish your self-esteem.

Bullying

In my experience, being bullied is one of the most common contributors to low self-esteem. If you've ever been bullied, you know firsthand how much impact it can have on you. The reason bullying has such a sizable impact is because it most commonly occurs during childhood and adolescence, precisely when identity formation is so crucial.

Bullying can cause a range of lasting psychological outcomes like anxiety, depression,[1] even post-traumatic stress disorder,[2] and of course low self-esteem.[3] Being bullied in school can impact a student's school performance by affecting concentration and willingness to participate in class. And in turn, unsatisfactory school performance can diminish a student's view of their intelligence or competence.[4]

When a person is bullied relentlessly, or by enough of their peers, they may start to internalize some of the messages they receive from their bullies. Children and adolescents primarily look to their peers for approval and acceptance, which makes them especially susceptible to developing feelings of inadequacy when their peers mistreat or reject them. As a result, they may adopt many of the harmful messages their bullies used to tease them. Internalization often occurs unconsciously, so someone might not even realize they're adopting the negative perceptions of others as their own.

If you've ever been bullied, it's highly likely that your experience affected your self-esteem. You may still have vivid memories of experiencing bullying even years later. It can really stick with you, so it's no surprise that it can shape your self-criticism, even in ways you might not recognize at first.

Parents/Caregivers

Parents and caregivers* have an enormous impact on their child's sense of self. Unfortunately, that impact isn't always positive. The intention of this section isn't to blame them for your low self-esteem. Most parents and caregivers are loving and caring and do their best, but parenting is hard, and nobody is perfect at it. Instead of blaming them for your low self-esteem, try to simply understand the role they may have played, even if it wasn't their intention.

Parents foster self-esteem in their children by giving affection, acceptance, and praise and showing interest in their child's achievements. When parents aren't warm and supportive to their children, their children may have difficulty acknowledging their own accomplishments and validating their own feelings. They might develop the belief that they aren't good enough.[5]

An important part of parenting is discipline. But parents who prioritize punishment and control over nurturance usually don't allow their children to make their own choices. As a result, their children might struggle to trust themselves and experience persistent self-doubt.[6] They also might become fearful of punishment when they make a mistake, which later on turns into harsh self-criticism.

---

* Not all family structures involve biological parents. For simplicity, I generally use the term "parents" in this section to refer to anyone in a significant caring role for a child.

Parents can also influence their children's self-esteem through modeling. Parents who struggle with their own self-esteem might model behaviors such as self-deprecation and reluctance to accept praise, which show their children that this is the way everyone should behave and view themselves.

Your parents or caregivers have had a major impact on your development as a person, and your self-esteem is an important part of that development. No matter your current relationship with them, consider the role they have played in how you interact with yourself (but do so without blame).

Unhealthy or Abusive Relationships

Like bullying, abusive relationships have a fairly straightforward impact on a person's self-esteem. Common practices in abusive relationships include belittling, insulting, or invalidating messages; statements or jokes about a person's inadequacy or undesirability; and even threats to a person's physical, social, or financial security. These behaviors directly impact your self-esteem, which is easy to see (at least from the outside).

What can be particularly insidious about abusive relationships is that they are rarely abusive 100% of the time. Often, the abuse is interspersed between periods of affection and support.[7] This can be a disorienting experience as the perceived lines between abuse and love begin to blur. Sometimes abuse can feel like just another form of love, but with disastrous effects on your sense of worth. It might become difficult to accept genuine support and affirmations from others because this type of support can feel confusing.[8]

Those who experience abuse can also internalize their experiences. They might begin to incorporate harmful messages from their abuser into their own self-concept and believe that they truly are incompetent, stupid, unattractive, or unlovable. The psychological impact of internalization usually lasts much longer than the abuse itself, which is why it can have such a profound impact on a person's self-esteem.

Another topic worth mentioning here is infidelity. Evidence shows that when a person is cheated on, the infidelity often impacts their self-esteem.[9] It can lead them to doubt their own worth or desirability or make them feel like they weren't good enough for their partner.

Unfortunately, unhealthy and abusive relationships aren't terribly uncommon. If you've ever been in an unhealthy relationship, take stock of the messages you received from those relationships and compare them to some of your most common self-criticisms. They might be strikingly similar.

Media

Research indicates that greater exposure to media tends to have a negative impact on a person's self-esteem.[10] People depicted in mainstream media often appear to have perfect bodies, perfect hair, perfect skin, perfect clothes, and perfect lives; they present impossible standards that most of us could never live up to. Advertisements constantly try to convince us that we're not good enough until we buy their products, and they often use guilt to manipulate consumer decisions.[11] While there are numerous ways the media can influence our self-esteem, this section will primarily focus on the impact of social media use.

Social media has a large impact on our self-esteem because it facilitates social comparison. Social comparisons can be either upward to someone we view as better off or downward to someone we view as worse off. Research shows that when using social media, people much more frequently engage in upward social comparison, and this bias causes them to feel inferior as a result.[12] In fact, heavy social media users are more likely to believe that others are happier and more successful and have better lives than them.[13] Even casual users are not immune to the harmful effects social media can have on self-esteem. Studies show that even 10 minutes on social media is enough time for a person to engage in at least one upward social comparison.[14]

Upward social comparison can happen in just about any context, but on social media comparison is usually more extreme. What you see when scrolling is usually the best possible portrayals of your peers because people are more likely to post statuses about positive life updates and experiences, and more flattering photos that are sometimes even digitally altered.[15] You're less likely to see their struggles and hardships. This can warp your perception of the lives of those around you, causing you to feel like your own life isn't as exciting or impressive.

We engage with different media channels almost constantly, maybe even more than we think. They're a huge force in our lives, so their ability to impact the way we think is hard to overstate. Consider how what you see in the media might be impacting how you interact with yourself and how your inner critic may have been hijacked by unhealthy messages.

Gender Norms

Studies on gender and self-esteem show that women tend to have slightly lower self-esteem on average than men.[16] However, much of the difference in self-esteem between men and women can be explained by sexism. Women, being lower on the social hierarchy of power than men, simply face more scrutiny in social situations than men, which can affect how they think of themselves. We'll explore impacts of power differentials and discrimination on self-esteem in more depth in the next section.

Just because women tend to have lower self-esteem than men doesn't mean men don't have their own struggles with self-esteem. Both genders experience pressure to measure up to the "ideal" standards of their gender, and the degree to which a person internalizes those pressures impacts their self-esteem. When a man experiences pressure to be obviously masculine, for example, he may feel the need to deny certain aspects of his personality that don't align with that standard. He may judge himself for the more feminine parts of his personality and feel that he doesn't measure up to what society thinks he "should" be.[17]

Transgender and nonbinary individuals also face gender pressures that impact their self-esteem. They're more likely to be stigmatized and face oppression on account of their gender, since it doesn't align with social norms.[18] They may struggle to accept and embrace who they are, as it's sometimes unsafe for them to be themselves. They may also internalize harmful societal messages about "normality" and feel that they don't fit in.[19] Being dismissed, rejected, or "othered" can have a profound impact on their self-perception.

Regardless of your gender, from the moment of birth, you're saddled with gender ideals that you're expected to measure up to. Consider how much the words of your inner critic echo the gender expectations society places on you.

Discrimination/Inequality

It's undeniable that we live within a social hierarchy, where certain people are afforded more power, representation, and opportunity than others. The topic of inequality is extremely broad, and individual experiences vary a lot. Regardless, being of lower social status can often result in harsh self-criticism, no matter your individual experience of inequality and discrimination.

Overt discrimination is one of the most tangible and obvious manifestations of inequality. Research shows that this type of discrimination has the largest impact on a person's self-esteem.[20] However, recent shifts in social norms have led to a decrease in overt discrimination, and in turn, microaggressions have become increasingly commonplace.[21]

Microaggressions are defined as "brief and commonplace daily verbal, behavioral, or environmental indignities (intentional or unintentional) that communicate hostile, derogatory, or negative slights and insults" toward a group of marginalized people.[22] Examples include having your competence doubted or authority challenged, being invalidated, having your individuality subverted in favor of stereotypes, being interrupted or patronized, having your identity be made into an insult like "that's so gay," and so many more.

The more a person is aware of microaggressions in their day-to-day life, the more their self-esteem tends to be negatively affected by them.[23] Because microaggressions are by nature subtle, and sometimes even well-intentioned, it can be difficult for a person who experiences them to get support from others or even seek restitution from the perpetrator.[24] Their experiences are often minimized, invalidated, and ignored. They may even start to doubt their own perception and view mistreatment and disrespect as normal.

It's not uncommon for someone who experiences microaggressions to internalize what they experience. If a person is viewed as less intelligent due to one of their demographic characteristics, for example, they might eventually start to view themselves as unintelligent. Over time the voices of their oppressors start to sound indistinguishable from their own voice. How might your experiences of inequality have influenced your inner critic?

Mental Illness (Stigma)

According to the National Institute of Mental Health, over 20% of adults in the United States live with a mental illness.[25] And low self-esteem is remarkably common among individuals with mental illness.[26] Having a mental illness doesn't by itself lead to low self-esteem. The relationship between mental illness and self-esteem is complex and outside the scope of this book. However, having a mental illness *and* being treated as less valuable than others because of it can certainly diminish a person's self-esteem. So this section will focus on stigma as a result of mental illness instead of mental illness itself.

Stigma occurs when the general public holds a stereotyped or inaccurate view of people with mental illness. For example, they may view mental illness as the result of a personal failing or believe that mental illness makes someone less competent. These inaccurate views of mental illness can result in unequal treatment, exclusion, discrimination, and more.[27] All of these experiences can impact a person's view of themselves and consequently their self-esteem.

Perhaps the most significant way this happens is through the process of internalization. As you can see by now, internalization is extremely common, and as social creatures, it's something we don't always have total control over.

Internalization of stigma can result in self-deprecation and feelings of inferiority, shame, incompetence, and brokenness.

People with mental illness experience stigma through both implicit and explicit messages. These messages are particularly harmful because certain mental illnesses like depression and anxiety can cause a negative bias in information processing. People with these mental illnesses are more prone to magnify any negative feedback or mistreatment they receive and minimize any praise or support. This has a profound impact on their self-esteem.

If you live with a mental illness, you may have experienced the effects of stigma in some way. Stigma can impact your relationships, your opportunities, and even your beliefs about yourself. It may have also played an important role in the development of your inner critic.

Trauma

Trauma can include a wide range of experiences. It doesn't just refer to victimization; even witnessing a traumatic event or experiencing prolonged adverse circumstances can fit the definition of trauma as well. Since it's not possible to cover each type of trauma separately in this section, I'll use generalizations to illustrate how traumatic experiences can affect your self-esteem.

Research shows that trauma often has a negative impact on survivors' self-esteem.[28] Trauma survivors (especially those who experienced violence) frequently take responsibility for what happened.[29] This is often a form of self-protection, because self-criticism gives the illusion of control over the situation. If you blame yourself for what happened to you, then the solution seems to be in your hands too. But that illusion of control comes at the expense of your self-esteem.

The amount of support you receive after the traumatic experience can significantly impact your self-esteem. Being supported when you're in need can improve your sense of worth. But if your experience is invalidated, minimized, or even denied, you may begin to doubt your perception of your own experience, feelings, or even your worthiness of support and acceptance.[30]

If you determine that a meaningful source of your harsh self-criticism is unresolved trauma, I encourage you to seek out treatment for your trauma from a licensed trauma specialist. While the information in this book is meant to help you build your self-esteem, it doesn't directly address trauma. Unresolved trauma can be a barrier to building your self-esteem and must be addressed before turning to self-actualization needs like self-esteem.

Capitalism

Capitalism is such a pervasive and influential global economic system that it's not a stretch to say it can impact how we think and behave. There's considerable evidence to show that people who live in capitalist societies suffer more mental health ailments than those living in less capital-centric economies.[31]

Capitalism upholds the idea that material wealth is synonymous with success and well-being. What seems to be extremely common in capitalist societies is ever-growing wealth inequality. Unfortunately, those who fall on the lower end of the wealth spectrum are led to conclude that their lack of wealth is due to a personal failure. So anyone who struggles financially is often assumed to be lazy or unskilled.

Under capitalism, much of our worth is based on our labor and productivity. The value of our time is literally quantifiable in the form of a wage, but that wage doesn't always reflect how hard we work or how much we contribute to society. For example, many of us consider teachers to be some of the most important contributors to our society, but unfortunately, that importance is often not reflected in their wages. Research shows that a person's economic situation can be a source of shame, particularly when they believe they're in a worse position than those around them.[32]

Some people, such as caregivers, who aren't part of the paid workforce may devalue their contributions to their household and society as a whole because there's no tangible earning attached to their labor. Not to mention, some people are unable to work due to illness, disability, or other factors. Since they don't directly contribute to the economy, capitalism vilifies them by calling them "freeloaders." Sometimes it seems that capitalism ensures that the highest earners also enjoy the highest self-esteem. Could that be by design?

The insidious ways capitalism impacts our day-to-day lives, and more specifically our self-esteem, can't be understated. From equating well-being with wealth to measuring worth with productivity, we adopt ideas from capitalism that don't end up benefiting us the way we hope. While it may have seemed a bit far-fetched at first, I urge you to consider whether the failings of capitalism have any relationship to your harsh self-criticism.

Individualistic Values

The culture you were brought up in has had a profound impact on your value system. Many of the world's cultures, especially in North America and Europe, uphold individualistic values. These values can sometimes be the basis for harsh self-criticism.[33]

Individualism prizes independence, assertiveness, free will, uniqueness, and autonomy. People in individualistic cultures tend to base their self-esteem on their competence and ability to reach personally defined goals. On the other hand, collectivism (the opposite of individualism) values enmeshment in a community, interdependence, connectedness, compromise, and adjusting your own desires to fit with the desires of the overall group. Therefore, people in collectivist cultures tend to base their self-esteem on their participation in and cohesion with their community.[34]

At first it seems that individualistic and collectivist cultures simply have different, but equally valid, conceptualizations of self-esteem. However, individualism's emphasis on competence and personal goals comes at a steep price. Since individualistic cultures champion self-sufficiency, they stigmatize asking for help. Those who ask for help are often considered weak, dependent, or even freeloaders. The need for occasional support is normal, but individualism makes receiving help seem abnormal or shameful.

Additionally, any hardship or adversity someone might experience within an individualistic society is frequently attributed to their own personal failings.[35] External factors are often ignored and blame is placed solely on the individual because they're thought to have free will and control over their own destiny. Despite everything in the world being more complicated than individual responsibility can explain, the individual's role is all individualism seems to be concerned with.

If you live in an individualistic culture, you likely "buy into" certain individualistic values on some level, whether you realize it or not. It's extremely difficult to completely subvert the influence of the culture you live in. Think about what individualism upholds and what it stigmatizes, then determine how closely your own self-criticisms match those priorities.

Cognitive Defusion: Untangling the Outside Force(s)

Now that you've identified one or more outside forces that have hijacked your inner critic, you can work on untangling them from each other. Shedding an unhelpful thought pattern is difficult when the thoughts seem integral to your identity. You can't take control of your inner critic if you can't discern the difference between your own thoughts and the thoughts you were conditioned to have. An effective way to approach this work is through a technique called cognitive defusion. It sounds deceptively complicated, but I promise it's not.

Cognitive defusion views a person as being initially "fused" to their thoughts.

In other words, it's difficult to distinguish thoughts from reality because our thoughts feel so real. Since our thoughts feel like reality, we usually accept our thoughts without much skepticism, viewing them as true, meaningful, and reliable. Cognitive defusion helps "defuse" you from your thoughts. Instead of proving a thought wrong, cognitive defusion helps you recognize that your thoughts are simply thoughts and aren't *necessarily* the truth.

Admittedly, there's a good amount of overlap between thoughts and reality, and the two aren't mutually exclusive. For example, when you think, *The roads are probably slippery since it's snowing outside*, your thought and your reality are probably in agreement. Cognitive defusion doesn't declare that your thoughts are untrue or unreliable. In fact, cognitive defusion isn't about evaluating the factual basis of your thoughts at all. It's about reminding yourself that just because you thought something doesn't mean it's true. It ensures your thoughts stay categorized in your brain as "just thoughts." They may or may not be true, but that's not the point right now.

Initially recognizing self-critical thoughts as just thoughts is a more manageable place to begin than trying to prove them wrong. The conventional response to self-criticism is to counter it with affirmations or evidence that they're not true. But our thoughts about ourselves are our most fundamental and deeply held beliefs. They're tightly fused to our sense of reality. So any attempt at challenging these thoughts initially feels like a betrayal—of who we are and even of the truth. Not to mention, the affirmation puts a lot of pressure on you to disagree. And if you don't disagree, that feeling can be crushing. That's why it's crucial to first create space between yourself and your thoughts before you focus on whether or not they're true. When a thought no longer feels so tightly intertwined with your reality, it's much easier to evaluate it objectively. Cognitive defusion gives you permission to disagree with your inner critic later (if appropriate). It also removes the pressure to take a firm stance.

You've probably tried proving your inner critic wrong before, and you know as well as anyone that approach just doesn't seem to work. Self-critical thoughts are stubborn, and when you respond to them by trying to disprove them, it often feels like you're lying to yourself. Anything you say to your inner critic has to be something you believe, or else you're just wasting your energy. For example, if you think *I'm stupid* and you respond to that thought by thinking *No, I'm smart*, you probably won't believe this new thought. If you did, you wouldn't have had the self-critical thought in the first place. But by defusing yourself from the thought by reminding yourself that it's just a thought, you're not lying to yourself. You're simply being careful not to give your thoughts more authority than they deserve.

At this point, try not to focus too much on disagreeing with your harsh self-criticism, and instead focus on defusing your thoughts from your reality. This will establish a foundation for later in the book when you'll learn how to evaluate the truthfulness or accuracy of your self-criticism. To defuse yourself from your thoughts, use this simple prefix to your thoughts:

I'm having the thought that _____ .

For example, imagine that your inner critic tells you that you're a failure. To defuse yourself from this thought, you can simply say to yourself, "I'm having the thought that I'm a failure." When you acknowledge that it's just a thought, you acknowledge that the thought may or may not be true. And that gives you the power to determine whether you want to accept the thought. But we'll get to that part later in the book. For now, all that matters is that you take power over your thought by acknowledging that it's not necessarily true simply because you thought it. It's ironic how much power and freedom can come from telling yourself that you *might* be wrong.

I'm a failure.
(sounds like a fact)

I'm having the thought that I'm a failure.
(sounds more subjective, so there's room for disagreement)

To take this exercise a little further, you can also call out the outside force that took over your inner critic. After reminding yourself that a thought is just a thought, think about where it came from. We aren't meant to beat ourselves up the way people with low self-esteem often do. When we're overly harsh toward ourselves, it's because we were taught to be that way. When you remind yourself that your harsh criticism stems from an outside force and doesn't belong to you, you can start untangling that force from your inner critic. Little by little, you can start taking back some control. When you experience harsh self-criticism, use this guide:

I'm having the thought that [self-critical thought]
because [outside force].

Here are some examples of what that might look like:

> I'm having the thought that I'm not good enough because my parents didn't usually celebrate my successes growing up.
>
> I'm having the thought that I'm stupid because my childhood bullies always said that to me.

Remember, the purpose of this technique isn't to project blame away from yourself and onto something or someone else, even though it might seem that way at first. That's why it's important to be clear about the difference between blame and understanding. There's a fine line between blame and understanding, but you have to be willing to tread that line instead of avoiding it.

For example, if your parents were a contributing factor to your inner critic, it's possible to understand the impact they had on you while also acknowledging they may not have done it on purpose. Maybe they had only the best intentions but just didn't know how to teach you to be kind to yourself. Or if bullies were an important outside force, it's possible to acknowledge their actions had a lasting impact on you while also recognizing they may have been hurting too, or they were acting out of immaturity. Understanding means discerning why something is happening while avoiding the moral judgment of right vs. wrong.

At the same time, you shouldn't look for excuses either. Taking the blame away from yourself still doesn't let you off the hook. Even if your harsh self-criticism isn't necessarily your *fault*, you're still responsible for doing all the work in this book. Excuses aren't helpful because they usually just lead to complacency. An excuse is a reason not to act, so be careful not to let your understanding become an excuse. Just because you aren't the problem doesn't mean you can't be the solution.

As you practice cognitive defusion with your own thoughts, you may find that sometimes it's all you need to dismiss a harsh or unhelpful thought. Reminding yourself that a thought is just a thought might strip it of its power over you and give you a sense of relief. Other times, cognitive defusion won't feel like enough. And that's okay. This isn't the final step—it's just the foundation for deeper work later on. For now, all you need to do is create some space between yourself and your thoughts, even if this space doesn't make the thoughts go away. In chapters 7 to 10, you'll learn techniques to evaluate and challenge the content of your self-criticism. This first step is a crucial part of the process, but it's not a quick fix.

Self-Compassion Exercise:
Defusing Your Self-Criticism

Which outside forces have hijacked your inner critic? It may be one or a combination of the above sources, or it may be something else altogether. All that matters is that the source isn't you. There's no right answer. As long as your response is genuine and shifts blame for your critical thoughts away from yourself, without blaming anyone or anything else, you'll develop a solid understanding of how your inner critic took on the harsh tone it has right now.

In the spaces below, indicate the source(s) of your negative self-talk. This will guide you in learning to separate your inner critic from yourself.

Source(s) of your harsh self-criticism:

_____

_____

_____

From this point on, when your harsh inner critic lobs nasty comments at you, remind yourself that they're not yours. There are several ways to do this, and there isn't a right way. Here are some examples of language you can use:

I'm having the thought that _____ because _____ .

That's what my abusive ex wanted me to think about myself.

Social media taught me to think this way.

That's a capitalistic mindset, not my own mindset.

My childhood bullies always used to say that to me.

Chapter 4

What's Not to Like?

When you think about who you are, what comes to mind? Ideally, you would think about a whole range of traits, including positive ones, negative ones, and even neutral ones. But if you have low self-esteem, your positive and neutral traits are probably completely overshadowed by weaknesses, mistakes, failures, and regrets. The painful conclusion seems to be the obvious one: that you're neither a good nor a likable person. To change that conclusion, you have to change the warped self-concept that made it inevitable.

This chapter will help you continue flattening your fun-house mirror by incorporating more positive traits into your self-concept. You'll learn how to acknowledge your strengths and integrate them into your self-concept. Depending on where your self-esteem is, that may seem like a tall order at first. But fear not—this chapter will lead you through the entire process systematically, and I promise it doesn't involve looking in the mirror and telling yourself that you're awesome.

This chapter will help you identify your positive traits *that already exist*, not teach you how to develop positive traits you don't have or force positive traits on yourself that you don't agree with. Remember, the point of flattening your fun-house mirror is to help you see an accurate reflection of yourself. You can't do that by lying to yourself. But you also won't benefit from minimizing or overlooking your positive traits. By the end of the chapter, you may be surprised by how many positive traits you can actually identify.

What Do You Like About Yourself?

I ask all my clients this in our very first session together. Often they give me a blank stare, like a deer in headlights, totally caught off guard by the question. Outside of job interviews, we don't get asked this question very much, so we usually don't give it much thought. Even when we're asked this question in an interview, we usually have a canned, maybe not-so-genuine response that we think the interviewer wants to hear. Usually, my clients aren't able to name more than a handful of things they like about themselves, and sometimes none at all. My clients have lots of great qualities, but that knowledge about themselves isn't always immediately available. They need a reference point, something to get them started. And you probably do too.

If I asked you to name every country in the world, you might struggle to do it (unless you're really good at geography). Even though you're probably familiar with the names of most countries and can recognize them when you hear them, that doesn't mean you can automatically recall them all on the spot. If you did try to name them all, you'd probably start with the countries you've visited before, or the ones you want to visit, or the ones you've heard the most about in the media. In other words, you'd more easily recall the most personally relevant ones. The same is true with your positive traits. When you're so used to overlooking your strengths and fixating on your weaknesses, a lot of your positive traits lose personal relevance and don't come to mind when you try to describe yourself.

To help you identify your positive qualities, I developed a list of 250 positive traits to act as that reference point. Instead of trying to identify traits on your own, you already have the traits in front of you; all you have to do is read through each one and determine which ones you think you have. Even if right now you can't think of a single thing you like about yourself, you might surprise yourself when you look through the list. There are probably some you've never even considered before.

Before you begin . . . a few words of caution. This list of positive traits is a helpful tool for building your self-esteem, but it's nothing more than that—it's just a tool. To avoid inadvertently misusing this tool, it's important to understand three common ways I see this happen:

- misunderstanding the purpose of the list
- focusing more on the traits you didn't choose
- equating your self-worth with your positive traits

Let's go through each one so you know what to avoid!

Misunderstanding the Purpose of the List

One way you might misuse this tool is believing that the traits you choose are objective measures of who you are. In reality, your self-concept is subjective. Just because you think of yourself a certain way doesn't necessarily mean you're right. So choosing your positive traits doesn't measure *who you are* but instead *how you think of yourself*. Remember, you're just starting the process of flattening your fun-house mirror. You might overlook some of your traits because you're not able to fully accept them yet. Just because you can't claim a trait doesn't necessarily mean it's not there. In the next chapter, you'll learn how to evaluate your standards for yourself, which hopefully will allow you to acknowledge some positive traits that you may not be able to yet.

Imagine that after reading through the 250 positive words, you choose 10. It might be easy to feel discouraged since it seems like you have so few positive traits. Now you feel even worse about yourself than you did before. But keep your mind open to the possibility that as you build your self-esteem, you'll be able to add more and more positive traits to your list. Not to mention, there's no predetermined goal for the number of traits you need to have a healthy self-esteem. This isn't a competition.

Focusing More on the Traits You Didn't Choose

For the purposes of this chapter, the only traits that matter are the ones you think you have. But it's hard not to give any weight to the traits you seem to lack. Some of my clients have described skipping over a trait as painful because they think not having that trait somehow makes them bad. Your harsh inner critic likes to use this tactic because it distracts you from your positive attributes and causes you to focus on your perceived deficiencies. While the presence of a positive trait is definitely a good thing, make no mistake: the absence of a positive trait is not a bad thing.

Remember, you don't need to be exceptional in order to like yourself. You aren't competing for the highest number of positive traits or the ideal combination of traits. You're learning to rethink the parts of yourself you may have overlooked before. If you get really bothered by a trait you think you lack, you can address it in chapter 11, which addresses your weaknesses. When your harsh inner critic tries to distract you by focusing on these traits, remind yourself that you'll get to them later, but for now you're only focusing on what you like about yourself.

Equating Your Self-Worth with Your Positive Traits

Finally, you might misuse this tool by believing that the traits you identify determine your self-worth. Remember, the only thing that should determine your self-worth is the fact that you exist. You are plain and simply worthy. That's it. Your self-worth has nothing to do with your personality or even what you like about yourself, so it's totally irrelevant here.

Identifying Your Positive Traits

Now it's time to identify all the positive traits you can. Feel free to add any traits that aren't in the following list. As you go, keep in mind that these are *traits*, not *identities*. Identities define you, and they can create a lot of internal pressure to measure up. Traits are just qualities you possess. You don't need to be the absolute personification of a trait in order to claim it.

Take your time as you read each trait, but don't agonize. When in doubt, just skip over a trait. The next chapter is about challenging your unfair personal standards, so you can address those traits then. For now, just choose the traits you can accept without too much internal debate.

To download a free copy of this list, visit rethinkyourself.info/worksheets or scan the QR code in the back of the book.

Accessible	Approachable	Candid	Complex
Accountable	Articulate	Capable	Concise
Active	Aspiring	Carefree	Conscientious
Adaptable	Assertive	Caring	Considerate
Adventurous	Athletic	Casual	Consistent
Agreeable	Attentive	Charismatic	Contemplative
Affable	Austere	Charming	Conversational
Alert	Authentic	Cheerful	Cooperative
Altruistic	Aware	Clearheaded	Courageous
Ambitious	Balanced	Clever	Courteous
Analytical	Benevolent	Collaborative	Creative
Animated	Bright	Companionly	Cultured
Anticipative	Bubbly	Compassionate	Curious
Appreciative	Calm	Competent	Daring

Decisive	Freethinking	Leisurely	Polished
Dedicated	Friendly	Logical	Polite
Deep	Fun-loving	Lovable	Practical
Detail-oriented	Funny	Loving	Precise
Dependable	Generous	Loyal	Principled
Determined	Gentle	Lyrical	Proactive
Dignified	Genuine	Mature	Productive
Diligent	Giving	Mellow	Professional
Diplomatic	Good-natured	Merciful	Protective
Direct	Goofy	Methodical	Punctual
Disarming	Graceful	Meticulous	Purposeful
Discerning	Gracious	Mindful	Quirky
Disciplined	Grateful	Modest	Rational
Discreet	Gritty	Moral	Realistic
Dutiful	Grounded	Multileveled	Reflective
Dynamic	Hardworking	Mysterious	Relaxed
Eager	Harmonious	Neat	Reliable
Earnest	Healthy	Non-authoritarian	Resilient
Easygoing	Helpful	Non-judgmental	Resourceful
Eccentric	Honest	Nurturing	Respectful
Efficient	Hopeful	Obedient	Responsible
Egalitarian	Hospitable	Objective	Responsive
Eloquent	Humble	Observant	Reverential
Empathetic	Humorous	Open	Romantic
Encouraging	Idealistic	Opportunistic	Scholarly
Energetic	Imaginative	Optimistic	Secure
Enthusiastic	Independent	Orderly	Selfless
Ethical	Industrious	Organized	Self-aware
Even-tempered	Innovative	Passionate	Self-sufficient
Excitable	Inoffensive	Patient	Sensible
Expressive	Inquisitive	Peaceful	Sensitive
Fair	Insightful	Pensive	Sentimental
Faithful	Intelligent	Perceptive	Serious
Fearless	Interesting	Persistent	Simple
Firm	Intuitive	Personable	Skillful
Flexible	Kind	Persuasive	Sociable
Focused	Knowledgeable	Planful	Soothing
Forgiving	Laid-back	Playful	Sophisticated
Forward-thinking	Leaderly	Pleasant	Spirited

Spiritual	Subtle	Thrifty	Unique
Spontaneous	Supportive	Tidy	Vibrant
Spunky	Systematic	Tolerant	Visionary
Stable	Tactful	Trusting	Warm
Steadfast	Talented	Trustworthy	Well-rounded
Stoic	Tasteful	Uncomplaining	Whimsical
Straightforward	Teacherly	Unconventional	Wise
Strong	Temperate	Understanding	Witty
Studious	Thoughtful	Undogmatic	
Stylish	Thorough	Unfaltering	

If you found this exercise to be uplifting and encouraging, great! You're well on your way to rethinking your self-concept and building a stronger self-esteem. On the other hand, if you found it to be challenging or uncomfortable, you're not alone. Identifying your positive traits might have emboldened your harsh inner critic to fight back. Some of my clients find this exercise to be not just uncomfortable but even loathsome. Not only does the exercise encourage them to engage in positive thinking about themselves (which they're not used to), but it brings up certain fears about what might happen if they think "too" positively of themselves. Here are some common reservations to identifying strengths. Maybe some will resonate with you.

Myth: Weaknesses Are More Important Than Strengths

I hear it all the time. "I need to focus more on my weaknesses than my strengths because that's how I grow as a person. I can't improve without knowing what's wrong." This statement is a half-truth, one that magnifies the importance of weaknesses and minimizes the importance of strengths. And that type of thinking leads to a warped self-concept. Remember, there's nothing wrong with acknowledging your weaknesses; in fact, acknowledging your weaknesses is good because it can lead to growth and progress. That's the true half of the statement. The false half is believing that weaknesses are more important than strengths. Building your self-esteem is impossible when you're reluctant to see the positives in yourself.

To demonstrate why this belief is unfair and hinders self-esteem development, I like to use this analogy. Imagine a classroom of 20 students. Half are excelling and half are struggling. Given that there's one teacher for 20 students, the teacher has to be strategic about how they allocate their time. The teacher might choose to allocate more of their time during a particular lesson to the 10 students who are struggling, since the other 10 students don't require much, if any, assistance. The teacher's decision means that they give unequal attention to each student. Does this mean the students who are excelling are less important than the ones who are struggling? Of course not! That's because there's a difference between attention and importance. The teacher can give more *attention* to certain students while maintaining that all students are equally *important*. The same idea applies to your strengths and weaknesses.

Even if you're laser-focused on self-improvement, that doesn't mean your strengths shouldn't get *any* attention. In order to have a strong self-esteem, you have to be willing to identify, acknowledge, and most importantly *utilize* your strengths. After all, your strengths are what get things done. They're the tools that help you achieve success and even improve on your weaknesses. They're incredibly important! When you ignore your strengths and let your weaknesses take center stage, the impact on your self-esteem is obviously detrimental.

Myth: If I Focus on My Strengths, I'll Become Complacent

People with low self-esteem often try to use harsh self-criticism as a motivator. They're afraid that giving themselves credit for what they're already good at will only lead to stagnation. The main problem with this reasoning is that research shows harsh self-criticism isn't nearly as effective as people often believe.[1]

Contrary to popular belief, harsh self-criticism can actually de-motivate you, and even result in a self-fulfilling prophecy. What you think about yourself has a profound influence on your actions. Generally speaking, a person's actions are in congruence with their self-concept. This means that thinking of yourself in positive terms is more likely to prompt positive behaviors than thinking of yourself in negative terms. For example, if you think of yourself as hardworking, then your actions will naturally reflect that. Your self-concept sets a standard of conduct that you're accountable to. On the other hand, if you think of yourself as lazy, you inadvertently give yourself permission to act in ways that align with your negative belief. After all, lazy people don't work hard, so why would you? Remember, this doesn't mean you should ignore your perceived weaknesses; it just means that focusing on your strengths isn't as threatening to your motivation as you might think.

This information may be in stark contrast to what you've been taught and how you currently approach your goals. If that's the case, you shouldn't expect yourself to adopt a new belief right away just because you read a few paragraphs on it. Give yourself some time to consider the possibility that harsh self-criticism isn't that effective. Your harsh inner critic will work hard to convince you that you must berate yourself in order to accomplish anything, but that's not really how it works.

Myth: If I Focus on My Strengths, I'll Become Arrogant

You've heard the adage "There's a fine line between confidence and arrogance." But it's not necessarily true; it's built on a false relationship between self-esteem and arrogance. These concepts have a lot less in common than most people think.

Self-esteem is your determination of whether and how much you like yourself, taking into account all factors, even your weaknesses and shortcomings. A person with healthy self-esteem can acknowledge that they're good and likable despite their imperfections. This doesn't mean they ignore their imperfections; it means they don't let their imperfections overshadow their positive qualities.

Arrogance, on the other hand, is a disregard for your weaknesses or limitations. It's an attempt to portray yourself as exceptional, without fault, and frankly, without self-awareness. In fact, arrogance is strongly related to low self-esteem because it's usually a form of overcompensation for your perceived weaknesses, a mask you put on to hide your imperfections out of a deep sense of shame.

Self-esteem is an entirely internal process (feelings of overall positivity toward yourself), but arrogance is largely an external process (a display of superiority or overinflated competence). Whereas self-esteem comes from beliefs and thoughts, arrogance is performative; its purpose is to impress others and/or hide insecurities. Confidence and arrogance aren't two points on the same continuum but, as many experts argue, entirely distinct concepts.[2]

Holding a personal value of humility, being careful not to tread into arrogance, is a commendable quality. If you're afraid you'll become arrogant by acknowledging your positive qualities, first recognize that this stance is virtuous. Next, remind yourself that the slippery slope from confidence to arrogance doesn't exist. Finally, keep in mind that feeling apprehensive about becoming arrogant is precisely what will prevent it from happening. Your concern about being pompous means you'll be acutely aware of anything that may be construed that way, and you'll be sure to avoid it.

Integrating Your Positive Traits Into Your Self-Concept

Building your self-esteem requires more than just identifying what you like about yourself. Your positive traits need to be integrated into your self-concept for them to really have an impact on your self-esteem. Most likely, not all the traits you identified in this chapter immediately came to mind when you asked yourself, What do I like about myself? That's because these traits aren't integral components of your self-concept right now. Maybe they've been overshadowed by your weaknesses, or maybe you never allowed them to be part of your self-concept in the first place. The rest of this chapter will teach you an exercise called active integration.[3] The process will help you add needed relevance to these traits so they feel like more concrete parts of who you are. To explain what active integration is, I'll use another analogy, this time about how we store information in our brains.

Imagine that your brain is a filing cabinet, with a file for every category of information you have knowledge of. There's a file for music lyrics, a file for how to do laundry, a file for the names of every person you know, and so on. The file for the things you like about yourself might be pretty sparse right now, and many of the traits you identified earlier aren't neatly filed away in their correct spot. The knowledge of your positive traits is filed away in your brain some- where, but it's not organized in a way that makes it easy to access. Instead, this knowledge is just shoved into the miscellaneous file where information tends to get lost. Part of building your self-esteem is organizing those thoughts so that knowledge of your positive traits is easier to access.

Now think about your file for things you don't like about yourself. This file is probably much more robust. You can access your negative traits fairly easily, and there are stacks of evidence to back each of them up. Everything in this file is meaningful, relevant, and readily accessible. Although you don't need to focus on this file in your brain just yet, it's important to note the differences between your positive traits file and your negative traits file so you can start to make them a little more equivalent.

One difference is that your negative traits file has more concrete information in it, with not only words to describe you but extensive evidence and examples that provide context. That robust evidence is what gives each negative trait more weight, relevance, and meaning. As a result, the information is more organized and easy to access. So to flatten your fun-house mirror, you have to find a way to mimic this organization style in your positive traits file.

This is where active integration comes in. Active integration simply entails attaching concrete data to abstract words. Remember my example about recalling all the countries of the world? The ones with the most personal relevance and meaning are the easiest to recall. When your positive traits are just words with little to no attachment to anything concrete, it's easy for them to get misplaced in your mental filing cabinet. By attaching memories, examples, and meaning to these positive traits, they become a part of how you see yourself and harder to deny when there's ample and compelling evidence to support them.

And repetition is your key to success. When you think about it, most types of change that are worth pursuing involve repetition. If you want to learn a new language, you'll have to work on it every day. If you want to ace a difficult test, you can't just review your study materials once. If you want to think of yourself more positively, you'll need to practice active integration repeatedly. There's just no other way.

Be careful not to compare yourself to others when you practice active integration. You don't need to prove that you're better than everyone else; you just need to show that you have good qualities. Self-esteem has nothing to do with comparing and everything to do with seeing yourself as good. Remember, thinking you're superior to others (arrogance) is usually associated with low self-esteem, not healthy self-esteem.

Also take care not to build your self-esteem on external factors like actions and accomplishments because these are fleeting and not integral to who you are. Not to mention, when you build your self-esteem on these factors, you risk allowing failures or mistakes to tear your self-esteem down. As a result, you end up with an ever yo-yoing self-esteem that you can never seem to get ahold of. Instead, build your self-esteem on your inherent traits. The examples (actions) you will identify in the active integration exercises to follow don't by themselves make you good or likable; they're just *evidence* of the good (positive traits) you already possess.

Active integration is not a coping skill. That means it's not meant to be used in direct response to your self-criticism. When your harsh inner critic starts acting up, stick to the techniques discussed in chapters 2 and 3 for now. Active integration is meant to be built into your daily routine to proactively foster a more positive self-concept. Now that you know what active integration is, let's start practicing it.

Self-Compassion Exercise:

Practicing Active Integration

In this section, you'll learn four methods to integrate your positive traits into your self-concept:

- linking traits to memories
- linking memories to traits
- demonstrating your positive traits in everyday life
- putting your traits on trial

I recommend trying each method on its own for a day or two, even if not all of them sound appealing at first. You might be surprised how they feel in practice. Once you've given each method a shot, stick with one or two that resonate most with you. It's very important that you take your time on this self-compassion exercise; this isn't a race. The more time you put into it, the more you'll get out of it.

Be prepared for your inner critic to make an unwanted appearance. As you take a closer look at each positive trait you chose, you might catch yourself starting to doubt them. If this happens, gently remind yourself that a few exceptions don't automatically disprove any of your positive traits. Even the most generous person in the world can sometimes be selfish. Even the funniest person in the world occasionally tells jokes that flop. You don't have to be perfect to claim a trait.

If after further reflection you change your mind on any given trait, feel free to remove it from your list. You don't need to force affirmations on yourself. This really should only be about traits you can accept somewhat freely. If you start having doubts about any positive trait, just know we'll address it in the next chapter, which will focus on your personal standards.

Method 1: Linking Traits to Memories

The most straightforward active integration method is to identify examples throughout your life when you've demonstrated each of your positive traits. This involves spending time reflecting on each of your traits individually. Some people prefer this method because it's thorough and detail-focused.

Trait: Organized

Examples:

1. I got a lot of compliments on how organized my workspace was in grade school.
2. I helped develop a more efficient organization system for supplies at work.
3. I was able to find something right away today because I kept it in its place.

It's best to identify examples from both the recent and the distant past. This highlights that the trait is permanent and integral to who you are. However, some of your traits may be relatively recent developments, and that's okay.

Don't put too much pressure on yourself to identify grand or exceptional examples. They can be remarkably minor. Remember, you're only trying to demonstrate that you *have* a trait, not that you're the best at it.

I recommend that you identify at least five examples per positive trait, but truthfully, the more examples you can identify the better. You don't have to come up with all five at once, though; you can skip around and identify a few examples for several traits at a time, then revisit the traits later to identify more. Just go about it in a way that makes the most sense to you.

In the spaces on the next page, choose one of your positive traits and identify at least five pieces of evidence for that trait. Then continue for all the traits on your list. Feel free to use a separate notebook or piece of paper if you run out of room!

To download a free copy of this worksheet, visit rethinkyourself.info/worksheets or scan the QR code in the back of the book.

Trait: _____
Examples:

1. _____

2. _____

3. _____

4. _____

5. _____

Trait: _____
Examples:

1. _____

2. _____

3. _____

4. _____

5. _____

Trait: _____
Examples:

1. _____

2. _____

3. _____

4. _____

5. _____

Method 2: Linking Memories to Traits

Some people prefer the first method because it's so thorough, while others find it tedious. If the latter is how you felt, you can reverse the order and achieve the same result with less attention to detail. Method 2 involves identifying positive things you've done, then identifying all the traits that were relevant in those instances. This method helps you cover a lot more ground than method 1 as you'll notice that many of your positive traits are often simultaneously relevant to a single situation.

Situation: Gave a stranger directions

Traits:

1. Approachable
2. Helpful
3. Knowledgeable
4. Friendly

Once again, the examples you come up with don't have to be exceptional. All that matters is that they're positive moments. Your accomplishments don't define your self-esteem anyway. They simply shine a spotlight on your positive qualities that were already there.

Just like in method 1, it's helpful to incorporate as much timeline variety as possible in order to demonstrate the longevity of your traits. And there's no limit to how many examples you can identify. Every day you might choose to identify one positive action from that day or the day before, as well as a positive action from your more distant past. You could theoretically continue this exercise every day for the rest of your life. This isn't an exercise you *complete* but one you *engage with*.

In the spaces on the next page, identify some good things you've done and the traits you used to do them.

To download a free copy of this worksheet, visit rethinkyourself.info/worksheets or scan the QR code in the back of the book.

Situation:

_____

_____

_____

Traits:

1._____

2._____

3._____

4._____

5._____

Situation:

_____

_____

_____

Traits:

1._____

2._____

3._____

4._____

5._____

Situation:

_____

_____

_____

Traits:

1._____

2._____

3._____

4._____

5._____

Situation:

_____

_____

_____

Traits:

1._____

2._____

3._____

4._____

5._____

Method 3: Demonstrating Your Positive Traits in Everyday Life

Some people prefer to be forward-thinking in their active integration rather than focus on past examples. To them, putting their energy into the future feels more intentional. That's what method 3 is for. To use this method, choose one or two positive traits each day, then be intentional about demonstrating them through your actions. For example, if you choose the trait Creative on a given day, make an effort to do something to express your creativity that day. The intention is to show yourself that you not only possess this quality, but that you're able to use it to bring added value to your own life or the lives of those around you.

Many people prefer this method because it gives them a sense of accomplishment when they set a daily goal for themselves and achieve it. Not to mention, if you use this method, you'll probably see some improvement in your occupational, social, romantic, or personal life. This method also might have the surprising outcome of demonstrating how naturally your traits come, since they're an integral part of who you are. It's not uncommon to forget about your trait for the day and realize in hindsight that you actually did use the trait without even realizing it.

Similar to the first two methods, your daily use of a trait doesn't have to be exceptional. It can be relatively minor. The only thing that matters is that you demonstrate to yourself that the trait exists and has relevance in your life.

In the spaces on the next page, write down one or two traits at the beginning of the day. Then at the end of the day, describe what you did to embody those traits.

To download a free copy of this worksheet, visit rethinkyourself.info/worksheets or scan the QR code in the back of the book.

Date: _____ Trait(s): _____
Action(s):

_____

Date: _____ Trait(s): _____
Action(s):

_____

Date: _____ Trait(s): _____
Action(s):

_____

Date: _____ Trait(s): _____
Action(s):

_____

Date: _____ Trait(s): _____
Action(s):

_____

Date: _____ Trait(s): _____
Action(s):

_____

Date: _____ Trait(s): _____
Action(s):

_____

Method 4: Putting Your Traits on Trial

Method 4 is made for people who like to argue. This method encourages you to imagine that your positive traits are on trial. The prosecution alleges that your traits are in fact negative, not positive. How would you justify the value and goodness of your traits to persuade someone to agree with you?

This method is also particularly useful for traits that have some stigma around them. For example, Sensitive seems like a negative trait to some. If you identified any traits that don't seem very positive at first, this method can help you get some perspective.

Ask yourself these questions to help get you started:
- What would the world be like if nobody had this trait?
  » What does this say about the value I contribute to the world?
- How has having this trait benefited me and/or others?

Trait: Sensitive

What would the world be like if nobody had this trait?

The world would be a cold, mean place.

What does this say about the value you contribute to the world?

By being sensitive, I bring empathy and compassion to the world.

How has having this trait benefited me and/or others?

Being sensitive helps me appreciate the emotion in writing, music, film, and other art.

When you think of ways a certain trait is valuable, you'll inevitably identify examples from your own life to support your argument. To some people, this feels like a more organic self-reflective exercise than the other methods.

In the spaces on the next page, choose one of your positive traits, then make a case for why that trait is important using examples from your own life.

To download a free copy of this worksheet, visit rethinkyourself.info/worksheets or scan the QR code in the back of the book.

Trait: _____

What would the world be like if nobody had this trait?

_____

What does this say about the value you contribute to the world?

_____

How has having this trait benefited me and/or others?

_____

Trait: _____

What would the world be like if nobody had this trait?

_____

What does this say about the value you contribute to the world?

_____

How has having this trait benefited me and/or others?

_____

Trait: _____

What would the world be like if nobody had this trait?

_____

What does this say about the value you contribute to the world?

_____

How has having this trait benefited me and/or others?

_____

Take the next several days, or even weeks, to carefully and thoughtfully practice active integration. You only need to make a small time commitment. The reflective methods (1, 2, and 4) require no more than 15 minutes of reflection per day. Method 3 is integrated into your day and requires essentially no time commitment other than recording what traits you chose and how you used them. If any of these methods particularly resonates with you, just focus on that one and use it as often as possible (daily is ideal, but we don't live in an ideal world, so do what you can).

There's no defined finish line. You can continue with active integration for as long as you choose. Success isn't measured by how much space you've filled in a notebook; it's measured by the confidence you feel in each trait as you practice the exercises. With active integration, the process is infinitely more important than the outcome.

Chapter 5

You're Doing Better Than You Think

Do you ever find yourself questioning your positive qualities? Maybe you started to doubt some of them while you did the active integration exercises in the previous chapter. Don't forget, your self-concept is subjective, so just because you think of yourself a certain way doesn't mean it's The Truth. And just because you won't allow yourself to claim a certain positive trait doesn't mean you don't have it. Since your self-concept is still warped at the moment, it's possible there's actually more good in you than you think. Depending on where you are with your self-esteem, that might sound unlikely. But by the end of this chapter, you might be surprised by how many of your positive qualities you've completely overlooked.

So far you've identified all the positive traits that you can claim somewhat confidently. But you probably noticed the determination wasn't always a simple "Yes, I have this trait" or "No, I don't." There were probably lots of other traits that you think you *might* have, but you're not quite sure if you can claim them. Maybe they're traits where you can identify just as much evidence to *refute* them as you can to *support* them, or traits that others have pointed out in you but you're not so sure you agree with. Whatever the case may be, your reluctance to claim certain positive traits may be rooted in your standards for yourself.

People with low self-esteem often have remarkably unfair standards for themselves. These standards are sometimes impossible to measure up to, and they end up reinforcing their low self-esteem. Imagine that you're taking a class with an extremely hard-to-please teacher. No matter how exceptional your work is, your teacher is never impressed and never gives you more than a C: "average." It's not that your work is bad, it's just that you'll always inevitably fall short of your teacher's impossible standards. In the same way, when you have unfair standards for yourself, it's hard to ever think of yourself as "good enough."

Unfair standards warp your fun-house mirror. They minimize your positive qualities so much that you end up overlooking many of them. For example, your loved ones may think of you as intelligent and hardworking, but because you don't meet your own elusive ideal, you disagree. Being unable to see your positive qualities for what they are only solidifies your negative beliefs about your capabilities. It may be difficult for you to even imagine what positive qualities might be hiding in that distorted reflection you see.

If your inner critic is loud enough, it seems like there's always something to criticize. Even your best isn't good enough because you could have done better. It seems that the only way to please your inner critic is to be perfect. But building your self-esteem isn't about being perfect; it's about learning to approve of your imperfect self. So long as your standards are unfair, you'll never be able to do that. This chapter will help you rethink the standards you use to evaluate yourself. You'll learn how to evaluate your positive qualities fairly, which is a crucial next step in flattening your fun-house mirror.

To be clear, high standards are not the problem—unfair standards are. In fact, high standards are a good thing, but only if they're attainable. To flatten your fun-house mirror, you may need to lower your standards slightly if they're impossible, but I won't ask you to abandon them entirely. Although it's technically true that rock-bottom standards are easier to measure up to, lowering your standards in this way isn't a healthy or realistic way to build your self-esteem. It's a half-baked strategy meant to trick you into liking yourself, and it won't get you very far. The goal here is to make your standards more fair and realistic, not to manipulate them so that you appear to be better than you really are.

All-or-Nothing Thinking

We're often unaware of just how unfair and unrealistic our standards are until we dig into them. Once we identify the distortions in our thinking, we can challenge and eventually change them. If you have unfair standards that keep your self-esteem low, it's probably due to a thinking error called all-or-nothing thinking, which involves dealing in extremes without any room for moderation.

All-or-nothing thinking tricks you into believing that if something isn't 100%, it may as well be 0%. It causes you to believe that there's a fine line between success and failure, when in fact there's a notably large gap between the two. If you engage in all-or-nothing thinking when it comes to identifying your positive traits, you may believe that if you can think of just one exception, then you don't measure up.

Nobody is immune to all-or-nothing thinking, and sometimes it can be pretty subtle. Imagine that you have a friend who you think of as compassionate, but you're surprised to learn they don't think of themselves that way. It seems so clear to you, an outsider, that this is a trait they possess. When you ask them why they don't think of themselves as compassionate, they respond, "I guess I can be compassionate sometimes, but I'm definitely not a saint." While at first their response simply sounds humble, it's evidence of their underlying belief that they can only claim a trait if they embody it to the fullest extent. The truth is, you don't need to be a saint to consider yourself compassionate. You just need to be . . . compassionate. The bar doesn't need to be so unattainably high. And if you're not careful, all-or-nothing thinking can erode your ability to accept any good in yourself at all.

In what ways does all-or-nothing thinking show up in your standards for yourself?

> When your inner critic points out exceptions to your positive traits, do you concede?
>
> Do you downplay the good in yourself because you know somebody out there is better than you?
>
> Do you allow a singular error or shortcoming to overshadow all of your positive traits and accomplishments?

All-or-nothing thinking can totally derail your efforts to build a healthy self-esteem. By upholding unfair and even sometimes impossible standards, you'll start believing that you have to be perfect in order to like or accept yourself. Your shortcomings and mistakes will feel threatening to your ego. If you want to flatten your fun-house mirror, you have to let go of all-or-nothing thinking.

To do that, let's take a look at the positive traits you're not sure you can claim.

Your [Kind of] Positive Traits

In the previous chapter, you identified the positive traits that definitely describe you. Now, you'll identify the traits that *kind of* describe you. These traits are a window into your personal standards. If you have unfair standards for yourself, they'll show up in your [kind of] positive traits. For any positive trait you can *kind of* but not fully claim, it's possible this is because of all-or-nothing thinking.

In this chapter, you'll learn some strategies to make your standards for yourself a little more fair and realistic, and you'll use your [kind of] positive traits as examples. The intention isn't for you to force any traits on yourself, though. It's up to you to decide what traits you want to claim. Maybe after examining your standards, you'll decide to claim a few more positive traits, and maybe you'll decide not to claim some of them after all. No matter where you land, the most important thing is that you give yourself credit for these positive qualities, whether they measure up to your standards or not.

Here is the same list of traits you were given in the previous chapter. Take your time and identify traits from the list you think you *kind of* possess. You can include any traits you want to possess but don't think you do, as well as any traits you removed from your list in the previous chapter due to self-doubt. After choosing your traits, you'll learn how to rethink your standards for yourself and keep flattening your fun-house mirror.

To download a free copy of this list, visit rethinkyourself.info/worksheets or scan the QR code in the back of the book.

Accessible	Appreciative	Bubbly	Companionly
Accountable	Approachable	Calm	Compassionate
Active	Articulate	Candid	Competent
Adaptable	Aspiring	Capable	Complex
Adventurous	Assertive	Carefree	Concise
Affable	Athletic	Caring	Conscientious
Agreeable	Attentive	Casual	Considerate
Alert	Austere	Charismatic	Consistent
Altruistic	Authentic	Charming	Contemplative
Ambitious	Aware	Cheerful	Conversational
Analytical	Balanced	Clearheaded	Cooperative
Animated	Benevolent	Clever	Courageous
Anticipative	Bright	Collaborative	Courteous

Creative	Focused	Laid-back	Pleasant
Cultured	Forgiving	Leaderly	Polished
Curious	Forward-thinking	Leisurely	Polite
Daring	Freethinking	Logical	Practical
Decisive	Friendly	Lovable	Precise
Dedicated	Fun-loving	Loving	Principled
Deep	Funny	Loyal	Proactive
Detail-oriented	Generous	Lyrical	Productive
Dependable	Gentle	Mature	Professional
Determined	Genuine	Mellow	Protective
Dignified	Giving	Merciful	Punctual
Diligent	Good-natured	Methodical	Purposeful
Diplomatic	Goofy	Meticulous	Quirky
Direct	Graceful	Mindful	Rational
Disarming	Gracious	Modest	Realistic
Discerning	Grateful	Moral	Reflective
Disciplined	Gritty	Multileveled	Relaxed
Discreet	Grounded	Mysterious	Reliable
Dutiful	Hardworking	Neat	Resilient
Dynamic	Harmonious	Non-authoritarian	Resourceful
Eager	Healthy	Non-judgmental	Respectful
Earnest	Helpful	Nurturing	Responsible
Easygoing	Honest	Obedient	Responsive
Eccentric	Hopeful	Objective	Reverential
Efficient	Hospitable	Observant	Romantic
Egalitarian	Humble	Open	Scholarly
Eloquent	Humorous	Opportunistic	Secure
Empathetic	Idealistic	Optimistic	Selfless
Encouraging	Imaginative	Orderly	Self-aware
Energetic	Independent	Organized	Self-sufficient
Enthusiastic	Industrious	Passionate	Sensible
Ethical	Innovative	Patient	Sensitive
Even-tempered	Inoffensive	Peaceful	Sentimental
Excitable	Inquisitive	Pensive	Serious
Expressive	Insightful	Perceptive	Simple
Fair	Intelligent	Persistent	Skillful
Faithful	Interesting	Personable	Sociable
Fearless	Intuitive	Persuasive	Soothing
Firm	Kind	Planful	Sophisticated
Flexible	Knowledgeable	Playful	Spirited

Spiritual	Subtle	Thrifty	Unique
Spontaneous	Supportive	Tidy	Vibrant
Spunky	Systematic	Tolerant	Visionary
Stable	Tactful	Trusting	Warm
Steadfast	Talented	Trustworthy	Well-rounded
Stoic	Tasteful	Uncomplaining	Whimsical
Straightforward	Teacherly	Unconventional	Wise
Strong	Temperate	Understanding	Witty
Studious	Thoughtful	Undogmatic	
Stylish	Thorough	Unfaltering	

Now that you've identified the traits that *kind of* describe you, let's take a look at whether you're evaluating yourself fairly. The first step is to separate these traits into two categories: one for traits that have an unhealthy extreme and one for traits that don't. To determine whether a trait belongs in the first category, ask yourself if it's possible to have "too much" of it. Lots of positive traits could fall into this category, like Persistent or Fearless. Let's take Persistent as an example. Generally speaking, persistence is a positive quality, but being "too persistent" can actually be a bad thing. Imagine if you were 100% persistent 100% of the time. You'd disregard other people's boundaries, you wouldn't take no for an answer, and you'd probably even be domineering so that you always got your way. Traits like these are interesting because they highlight that there can be too much of a good thing, which means all-or-nothing thinking will lead you in the wrong direction.

The second category is traits that do *not* have an unhealthy extreme. There can never be "too much" of them. These include traits like Ethical or Punctual. Could you imagine someone saying to you, "You're too punctual"? Of course not! Because that trait just doesn't have a bad side. These traits are categorically different than the traits with an unhealthy extreme, so you have to approach them a little differently. It's trickier to let go of all-or-nothing thinking with these traits, but it's not impossible!

Take some time to look through the traits you just chose and put them into their respective categories. It's a subjective determination, so there are no right or wrong answers. That's why I didn't categorize them for you. You should decide what makes the most sense for yourself. So take some time to decide which of your [kind of] positive traits could have a healthy extreme and which ones don't. Keep in mind you're not determining whether you personally take any of these traits to an extreme, just whether the traits would still be positive if you did.

In the next section, you'll find two exercises to help you rethink your standards for yourself—one for each category of trait in your list. These exercises will help you avoid all-or-nothing thinking by challenging your assumptions about what's acceptable and exploring the space between "all" and "nothing."

Rethinking Your Standards: Traits with an Unhealthy Extreme

Since you've already determined that there are positive traits that can actually be considered negative when taken to 100%—and therefore it would be unreasonable to aim for 100%—you've already dismantled all-or-nothing thinking (but that doesn't mean you're done yet)! By acknowledging this, you've already taken immense pressure off yourself to be perfect . . . because that would, ironically, be a bad thing. If you were *completely* persistent, for example, that in fact would be less desirable than if you were *kind of* persistent.

Let's do an exercise to take a closer look at how to form reasonable standards for these traits. To show how to do this exercise, I'll use Persistent again as an example. Even though persistence is a good quality, someone who's 100% persistent 100% of the time is probably also incessant and stubborn. All-or-nothing thinking would have you believe that you must shoot for 100%, but you now know that for some traits this standard is unhelpful. So if 100% isn't the goal, then what is? We have to start by determining the optimal level of persistence. Again, this determination is subjective, so there's no right or wrong answer. And admittedly, reducing an optimal amount of persistence down to a singular percentage point is an oversimplification of a complex idea. The purpose of using percentages isn't to make a definitive determination but simply to explore the space between "all" and "nothing." Therefore, any percentages you assign might not feel like completely accurate depictions of reality, and that's okay. They're tools, not laws. Complete accuracy isn't the point, so don't stress too hard about getting it exactly right. If percentages aren't your thing, you could also create a spectrum from "not persistent" to "completely persistent" and determine where on that spectrum optimal persistence likely falls. No matter what determinations you make, you'll still achieve the goal of rethinking your standards.

For this example, I'll say that 70% persistence is the optimal level of this trait. This is (in my opinion) the highest amount of persistence someone can demonstrate *and still have persistence be considered positive*. I consider anything above 70% persistent to be "too persistent" and therefore unhealthy.

It's totally subjective, and that's okay. This is just a tool for exploration, not a scientific analysis.

Persistent

At this point, I've decided that the gold standard of persistence isn't actually 100% but a much more humble 70%. In a school setting, this would be a C-. Doesn't that make persistence feel like a more attainable trait? Conceiving of it like this helps us scale back our all-or-nothing thinking standards by relieving the pressure to be perfect. Isn't it weird to think that you don't want any better than a C- on this one?

The exercise doesn't end here, though. We also have to account for the human condition—humans are imperfect and we can't *always* be an optimal amount of anything. We can strive for an optimal 70%, but we can't realistically *expect* it. We have to give ourselves the grace to be imperfect, otherwise nothing we ever do will feel "good enough." Perfection will always be just out of reach. Since I determined that 70% is my optimal level of persistence, there must be an acceptable range of persistence below 70% to account for human error and imperfection. Again, this range is for you to decide, but I'll set my own range at 60% to 70%. I refer to this as "ideal persistence." This means that exhibiting somewhere between 60% to 70% persistence, on average, is my personal standard. But that doesn't mean anything under 60% is *passive* or *weak* either. It just means that anything lower than 60% hasn't met my personal standard for persistence. Look at how large the gap between 0% and 60% is. While 55% may not fall within the ideal range, for example, it's certainly not insignificant. Be careful not to equate anything less than "ideal persistence" with its opposite. That would involve all-or-nothing thinking!

Persistent

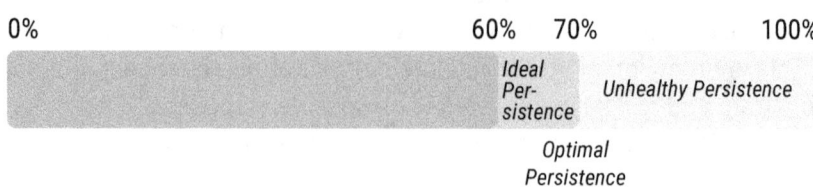

Now that I've determined a realistic personal standard for persistence, I can fairly assess my own persistence to determine whether this is a trait I possess. Before getting into the details of what's truly ideal, it may have been easy to believe that 100% persistence is the goal. All-or-nothing thinking would have me believe that 60% to 70% isn't good enough. But now it's clear how unfair that standard was. It may be surprising to acknowledge that 60% of a trait is considered "ideal." After all, 60% is a D-! But acknowledging that 60% is good enough is an important way to embrace the good in yourself despite being imperfect. Where would you place yourself on this persistence scale?

After determining a realistic standard of persistence (or any other trait), you have an optional step and an imperative step. If you determined that you fall within the ideal range of persistence (according to your own percentage estimates, not mine), you have the option to choose to claim Persistent as one of your positive traits. If this exercise convinced you to integrate an additional positive trait into your self-concept, that's great! But that's not the point of this exercise. Remember, this was the optional part.

The imperative step is to recognize that no matter where you put yourself on the scale, even if it's below your ideal range, you must give yourself credit for whatever amount of this trait you do have. This exercise is meant to help you let go of all-or-nothing thinking, a.k.a. believing that if you don't fall within the ideal range of a certain trait, you might as well be its opposite. For example, if I rated myself as 50% persistent according to my own scale, all-or-nothing thinking might cause me to feel that I'm *resigned*, which is not only irrational but also very unfair.

Giving yourself credit for partially possessing a positive trait doesn't mean ignoring the ways you can improve on that trait. It simply means acknowledging that you have *some amount* of that trait. It means that you're persistent at times, maybe even most of the time. It means that you care about being persistent. You can give yourself credit for coming close to the mark *and at the same time* strive to do better. You don't have to choose one or the other!

In this example, I should give myself credit for at least being 50% persistent. After all, it doesn't need to be a defining trait of my identity for me to recognize that I possess it in some respect. In fact, most people possess some amount of nearly all the positive traits on the list. Your standards are what determine whether you can claim it or not. And although you don't need to claim every positive trait to have a strong self-esteem, you should give credit (even a tiny amount) where it's due.

Self-Compassion Exercise:

Rethinking Your Standards (Traits with an Unhealthy Extreme)

Now you can do this exercise on your own, using your own traits and percentages. You may end up claiming a new positive trait, but either way, you can practice giving yourself credit for partially possessing a positive trait.

Step 1: Choose a [kind of] positive trait to examine your standards on.

Remember, it should be a trait with an unhealthy extreme. Determine the optimal amount of that trait and draw a line at the approximate percentage (by definition, this will be less than 100%).

Step 2: Give yourself grace by identifying an ideal range for this trait rather than a strict cutoff.

Keep in mind that you're human and won't always meet the optimal mark. Doing this acknowledges the space between "all" and "nothing."

Step 3: Determine where you believe you fall on your scale for this trait and note whether you fall within or outside the ideal range.

If you believe you fall within the unhealthy range, you may remove this trait from your list and address it in chapter 11 on rethinking your negative traits. If you determine that you fall within the ideal range, you may transfer this item to your list of positive traits if you wish, but you don't have to. There's no need to force it on yourself if it still doesn't feel right.

Step 4: No matter where you fall on the continuum (unless you fall within the unhealthy range), give yourself credit for possessing some amount of that positive trait.

It doesn't have to be a defining feature for you to recognize that you have some of it.

There's space on the next page for you to complete this exercise for five traits, but I encourage you to evaluate your standards for each of your [kind of] positive traits in this category.

To download a free copy of this worksheet, visit rethinkyourself.info/worksheets or scan the QR code in the back of the book.

Positive Trait: _____

0%   100%

Positive Trait: _____

0%   100%

Positive Trait: _____

0%   100%

Positive Trait: _____

0%   100%

Positive Trait: _____

0%   100%

Rethinking Your Standards:
Traits Without an Unhealthy Extreme

Now that you've learned how to rethink your standards using traits with an unhealthy extreme, we'll modify the exercise to apply it to traits that don't have an unhealthy extreme. Since there's no such thing as "too much" for these traits, the "optimal" amount will always be 100%. It's a bit more difficult to let go of all-or-nothing thinking with these traits, but it's not impossible. This exercise just requires a bit more nuance than the last one.

I'll use the trait Ethical as an example because I think most people would agree that there's no such thing as being too ethical. Therefore, the optimal amount of this trait is technically 100%. Setting the optimal amount below 100% isn't an option like it was in the previous exercise.

Ethical

0%   100%

Optimal
Ethics

But just like the previous example, we have to account for human error. Because of human error, 100% ethical, or any other positive trait, is impossible. We may strive to be 100% ethical, but we're imperfect and inevitably make mistakes. Nobody ever has or ever will hit the 100% mark 100% of the time (and neither will you). No matter how hard we try, sometimes we make unethical decisions. And even just one unethical decision makes a person less than 100% ethical. "Optimal" is simply an unattainable standard, and it's unfair to expect it of yourself.

When you're aiming for 100%, which is impossible, you're just setting yourself up for failure. And when you're never able to measure up despite your best efforts, you risk developing a sense of inadequacy. This is why all-or-nothing thinking can be so detrimental to your self-esteem. Aiming for perfection when perfection is impossible is profoundly unfair.

Acknowledging that 100% is impossible is a good first step to dismantling all-or-nothing thinking. Since nobody can be 100% ethical (all), it's irrational to then assume everyone is 0% ethical instead (nothing). All-or-nothing just doesn't make sense when you really think about it. Acknowledging this will help alleviate the pressure to be perfect, just in a different way than the previous exercise did.

If being 100% ethical is unattainable, it's helpful to start by determining the highest level of ethics someone can realistically attain, taking into consideration human error and scaling back the expectation of perfection. Again, this is subjective and highly complex, but I'll determine the amount to be 90% for this exercise. This percentage represents the highest amount of ethics a person can ever possibly achieve. Any amount above 90% is impossible (in my opinion).

Ethical

Attainable Optimal

By sliding the target back by even just 10%, measuring up to this standard feels a tiny bit more attainable. This is a more reasonable way to determine whether you can consider yourself ethical since it doesn't require you to meet an impossible standard. Still, it's important to recognize that 90% ethical refers to the absolute most ethical person who has ever lived. It's an exceptional amount of this trait. Even though I might consider it technically possible to attain this level of ethics, it's still not a very reasonable expectation to have for myself, or anyone else for that matter.

It's important to view this trait and others as a range rather than a binary. That's how you undercut all-or-nothing thinking. Despite your best efforts, you probably can't be the highest possible amount of any positive trait *all the time*. If you don't give yourself the grace to be imperfect, you're practically guaranteed to never measure up. Here, you need to give yourself a grace range, which allows for mistakes while still leaving you with the ability to consider yourself ethical. I'll set my own grace range at 70% to 90%. This is my personal standard of ethics. Again, this doesn't mean that anyone who falls below 70% is unethical, just that they may not want to claim this trait. Note how large the gap between 70% and 0% is on the diagram below. It would be extremely unreasonable to equate any level of ethics below 70% with the opposite (unethical) as all-or-nothing thinking might cause you to do.

Ethical

0%   70%   90% 100%

Grace Range

Attainable Optimal

Before doing this exercise, you may have assumed that striving to be 100% ethical is the gold standard you should measure yourself against. But as you can see now, perfection is not the standard, and it's perfectly okay to claim the trait even if you fall lower than 100%. Where would you place yourself on the ethics scale?

After completing this exercise, you have an optional step and an imperative step. You may determine that where you fall on the scale is within the grace range (according to your own estimates) and therefore opt to claim this trait for yourself. If so, you now have one additional positive trait to add to your list! However, if you determined that you fall outside the grace range (or even if you fall within it but still don't want to claim the trait), there's no requirement that you add the trait to your list of positive traits. This part is optional. There's no magical number or combination of positive traits you must claim in order to have a strong self-esteem.

Whatever you decide, you absolutely must give yourself credit for having some amount of this trait. That's the imperative step. You must recognize that even if you don't meet your own standard, it doesn't automatically make you the opposite of that trait. It just means you're human and have some improvements to make. Being perfect isn't the goal; seeing the good in yourself (even when you fall just short) is.

Self-Compassion Exercise:

Rethinking Your Standards (Traits Without an Unhealthy Extreme)

Now try this using your own traits and percentages. Follow the steps below to rethink your standards. You may end up claiming a new positive trait, but either way, give yourself credit for partially possessing a positive trait.

Step 1: Choose a [kind of] positive trait to examine your standards on.

Remember, it should be a trait without an unhealthy extreme. Since the optimal amount of this trait is already set at 100%, start by identifying and marking the achievable amount for each trait, taking into consideration that we're human and we won't meet the optimal mark every time (this will be somewhere below 100%).

Step 2: Account for human error and imperfection by identifying a grace range, with the achievable amount at the top of this range.

Doing this acknowledges the space between "all" and "nothing."

Step 3: Determine where you believe you fall on each continuum and note whether you fall within or outside the grace range.

If you determine that you fall within the grace range, you may transfer this item to your list of positive traits if you wish, but you don't have to. There's no need to force it on yourself if it still doesn't feel right.

Step 4: No matter where you fall on the continuum, give yourself credit for possessing some amount of a positive trait.

It doesn't have to be a defining feature for you to recognize that you have some of it.

There's space on the next page for you to complete this exercise for five traits, but I encourage you to evaluate your standards for each of your [kind of] positive traits in this category.

To download a free copy of this worksheet, visit rethinkyourself.info/worksheets or scan the QR code in the back of the book.

Positive Trait: _____

0%   100%

Positive Trait: _____

0%   100%

Positive Trait: _____

0%   100%

Positive Trait: _____

0%   100%

Positive Trait: _____

0%   100%

Chapter 6

Are You Defending Your Negative Beliefs?

Your beliefs about yourself are foundational to your self-esteem. Some of them contribute to a warped self-concept. As you know, you need to rethink those beliefs so you can see yourself in a flat mirror, so to speak, without the influence of harsh and unfair self-criticism. You've already done a lot of work to integrate more positive traits into your self-concept, but have you ever considered how you might actually be defending certain negative beliefs about yourself?

This chapter is all about overcoming a common barrier to developing a healthy self-esteem: defensiveness. You may not realize it, but you might actually be defending your negative beliefs about yourself almost daily, and even out loud. When you assert that these beliefs are true and unwavering, you inadvertently reinforce them. As long as you continue defending your warped self-concept, there will never be a compelling reason to rethink it.

To build your self-esteem, you have to change the way you think about yourself. But to do this, you have to question the accuracy of your self-critical thoughts and beliefs, evaluate their logic, and sometimes conclude that they were inaccurate, unfair, illogical, or simply wrong. And we don't like to be wrong.

How do you feel when someone tells you you're wrong? Maybe you feel uncomfortable, embarrassed, defensive, or even inferior. Even if you're challenged in a constructive, supportive, and non-aggressive way, you probably can't help but feel at least some negative emotions. That's just a normal human reaction to being challenged. So when you challenge your warped self-concept—and the corresponding deeply held beliefs about yourself that make it up—you'll likely experience these exact feelings, except in a more personal way than just being wrong about external things like math or history. Your beliefs about yourself have been forming for most of your life, and right now many of those beliefs are negative. When someone challenges them by pointing out the good in you (or even if you try to challenge your own negative beliefs by finding the good in yourself), it probably feels a little (or a lot) uncomfortable. Some of my clients have even described this type of challenge as a violation.

Most people don't have their beliefs about themselves challenged very often. But for someone with low self-esteem, challenges to their self-concept come regularly, in the form of compliments. After all, a compliment is nothing more than positive feedback, which often feels a bit foreign to someone with low self-esteem. For many of my clients, even the thought of a compliment is enough to send shivers down their spine. They receive compliments the same way a vending machine receives a wrinkly dollar bill—they stubbornly reject them. The reason compliments can feel so uncomfortable is because they call into question your negative beliefs about yourself by highlighting that someone else disagrees.

Imagine that you believe you're lazy, and someone (perhaps without even knowing how you feel about yourself) says they admire how much work you put into something. You might feel a rush of defensiveness and discomfort. After all, who knows you better than yourself, right? You may feel that they're only trying to be nice and don't really mean it; or worse, you may feel like a fraud for tricking them into believing something about you that isn't true. So what do you do? Out of defensiveness, you might minimize the compliment ("It was no big deal"), deflect it ("I'm definitely not as hardworking as you are"), or even argue that the compliment is wrong ("No, I'm not, I'm lazy"). Of course, part of this may be cultural; sometimes we're expected to respond to compliments with humility so we don't let our ego become inflated by praise. This is especially true in the Midwest, where I grew up and currently live and practice. Here, it's an unwritten rule that you must respond to compliments by deflecting. However, for individuals with low self-esteem, there's usually more at play than just social or cultural expectations—their self-concept is being challenged. When you receive a compliment that contradicts your self-concept, you probably experience discomfort. To alleviate your discomfort, you have to either do mental work to agree with the compliment or rationalize it out of existence. This discomfort is referred to as cognitive dissonance. It's the feeling someone gets when they experience two things, such as beliefs, thoughts, actions, or feelings, that contradict each other. Existing in a state of dissonance for long periods of time can feel very uncomfortable, even threatening, so we often try to resolve the contradiction by adopting a new belief, rationalizing, or denying.

This is why accepting compliments is so important to your work on building your self-esteem. Since compliments cause cognitive dissonance, you have a choice in how to resolve that internal conflict—work toward adopting new beliefs by allowing the compliment to slowly chip away at your negative view of yourself, or continue to deflect. But the more you deflect, the more you confirm those beliefs are true and therefore resistant to any challenge. Is the work of deflecting really worth doing for the sake of avoiding internal discomfort?

The Backfire Effect

Deflecting and minimizing compliments may seem innocuous on the surface, but when someone with low self-esteem does it, they're actually defending their warped self-concept. When you're confronted with a challenge to your self-concept, your beliefs about yourself are called into question, which creates cognitive dissonance—*Are my beliefs about myself true, or is the compliment true?* The easiest and least uncomfortable way to resolve this dissonance is to reject the compliment. Rejecting involves minimal internal work, mainly because it doesn't require you to consider possibilities that you didn't previously see, and more importantly, you don't have to admit that you're wrong about yourself. When you reject a compliment, however, you're essentially defending, preserving, and reinforcing your warped self-concept. By digging in your heels and declaring that the compliment is simply untrue, you're asserting that your negative beliefs about yourself cannot and should not be challenged. And you can probably see how repeating this enough times starts to make a pretty compelling case that your warped self-concept is objective truth. Deflecting the compliment helps you avoid discomfort, but it also entrenches you in harsh self-criticism.

Simply put, when you shield your self-concept from challenges, you reinforce it. When you don't allow any evidence to challenge your beliefs, you eventually reach the conclusion that your self-concept is accurate. The more you deflect compliments, the stronger and more rigid your warped self-concept becomes.

Most people don't like to have their beliefs challenged, and coming to the defense of our beliefs, whether they're true or not, is a very common reaction to that challenge. Research shows that people tend to process information in ways that reinforce their pre-existing beliefs.[1] This means when someone is confronted with information that contradicts what they already believe, the new information may inadvertently strengthen their pre-existing belief. This phenomenon is commonly referred to as the backfire effect. It usually shows up in topics that involve misinformation, particularly around political issues. For example, research has shown that when a person who is concerned about side effects of a vaccine is shown evidence that the vaccine is safe, they may paradoxically become less willing to take the vaccine.[2] And when they actively argue against a viewpoint or piece of information that contradicts their own views, even if their pre-existing beliefs are factually incorrect, the very act of defending their beliefs can strengthen them.[3]

The backfire effect seems irrational, but nobody is immune to it. In fact, you might now be able to recognize times when a compliment you received actually caused you to believe more strongly that the opposite was true. To build a stronger self-esteem, you have to prevent compliments from inadvertently strengthening any negative beliefs you have about yourself. Fortunately, there are also ways to overcome the backfire effect. The most impactful way is to simply be aware of it. Having self-awareness about this process allows you to think more critically and objectively about how your beliefs conflict with new information you receive. And now that you're aware of the backfire effect, you can work toward overcoming its potential negative effect on your self-concept.

The Role of Discomfort in Change

I hate to break the bad news, but dismantling defenses to your warped self-concept will involve some discomfort. It will involve taking in observations that feel threatening to your pre-existing beliefs and welcoming the cognitive dissonance they create. However, for people with low self-esteem, acknowledging their warped self-concept in any way is often uncomfortable. Receiving feedback that contradicts how you see yourself may cause you to feel defensive and uncomfortable. On the other hand, if someone were to confirm what you already believe about yourself—that you're stupid, unlikable, or unsuccessful, for example—you would probably feel crushed.

This paradox is difficult for someone with low self-esteem to escape from. When their beliefs are challenged, they feel discomfort; when their beliefs are confirmed, they feel devastated. No matter what, they experience discomfort. So as you start working on your self-concept, prepare to feel some level of discomfort. But remember that it's up to you which type of discomfort you'd rather experience: the discomfort of being confronted with the possibility that what you think of yourself is wrong, or the possibility that you may be right.

To understand this point a little better, imagine your life without any compliments. From now on, nobody gives you any positive feedback. To some, this may bring a huge sense of relief . . . at first. But imagine, on any occasion, big or small, never getting any indication that others think positively of you. Nobody congratulates you when you finish school or get a promotion. Nobody tells you how great you look on your wedding day. Nobody compliments the Beef Wellington you absolutely nailed. You never hear that you've provided any value to anyone's life. How miserable would that be? It would deliver a huge blow to your self-esteem. So even if compliments make you uncomfortable, try to recognize how important they are by imagining what life would be like without them.

How to Respond to Compliments

People with low self-esteem often find it extremely challenging to accept compliments. If you feel that way, don't worry—in this chapter you'll learn a step-by-step approach to responding to compliments that minimizes the potential for overwhelming feelings. You won't be thrown to the wolves. Instead, you can take a more gradual approach.

You'll proceed through what I call the ABCs of compliments: accepting, believing, and considering. These stages will be your guide as you slowly work toward building more engagement with compliments. Each stage in the process goes a little deeper and requires a little more mental effort than the last. It's best to focus on one stage at a time and only move on to the next stage when you feel ready.

Stage 1: Accepting Compliments

The first stage of responding to compliments requires the least amount of internal work. In this stage, all you need to do is accept the compliment. Initially this might sound like a pretty big ask. But maybe you believe that accepting compliments is a larger and more meaningful task than it actually needs to be. To ease your apprehension, here's what it looks like to accept a compliment:

> Person 1: "You did a great job on that presentation."
> Person 2: "Thanks. I appreciate the feedback."

That's it. That's all that's required at this stage. We'll build on it later.

Now, you may be thinking, *That's it? It's not that easy!* This is a response I get a lot, often because of assumptions about what is required to accept a compliment. So to be clear about what accepting compliments really means, here's what it does *not* mean.

- **Accepting compliments does not mean you have to mean it when you say "thank you."** On the inside, you may be wailing in discomfort. You may secretly wish the person hadn't said anything. You may be dying to deflect. But you don't.
- **Accepting compliments does not mean you have to agree with what the person said.** You may feel an intense desire to correct the person because it feels like an injustice to let them go on believing something that's wrong. You may have a thousand rebuttals to their compliments. But you keep them to yourself.
- **Accepting compliments does not mean you're arrogant.** There's nothing arrogant about saying "thank you" when someone says something kind. In fact, a thank-you is simply the most polite way to respond.

If you're used to minimizing or deflecting, then accepting compliments will probably cause some cognitive dissonance. After all, your words (thank you) will probably be in stark contrast to your thoughts (that's not true)—that's the very definition of cognitive dissonance! Just remind yourself that at this stage, you don't have to do any of the internal work yet; accepting is purely an external process. At this point in the process, don't worry about changing any of your beliefs about yourself; all you have to do is accept compliments without deflecting. You're trying to build a new healthy habit before you get into any of the internal stuff. You're taking one step at a time toward breaking down the defenses that preserve your warped self-concept.

Self-Compassion Exercise:
Accepting Compliments

Before moving on to the next stage, take some time to focus on this one. Don't start on stage 2 until you've mostly moved past the discomfort of simply accepting compliments. If you prefer quantitative indicators, my rule of thumb is that when compliments cause discomfort at a 3 or less on a scale of 10, you're ready to move on to the next stage. You might already be at this point, so you don't have to commit much effort here; just check this stage off your list and go to stage 2. On the other hand, accepting compliments may feel so uncomfortable that you wonder how you'll ever make it to stage 2. But if you make it a habit to accept compliments despite the discomfort, eventually you'll grow more accustomed to it and it won't feel as uncomfortable. This process is called habituation, which is a person's tendency to acclimate to an initially uncomfortable or anxiety-provoking stimulus after repeated exposure to it. It's the mechanism that underlies exposure therapy, which challenges a person to face their fears repeatedly and systematically in order to overcome them.

Getting comfortable with compliments may take some time, and the process is different for everyone. Some may start feeling more comfortable after a week, and others may take several weeks before they notice any change. Ultimately, what you get out of this exercise depends on what you put into it. The temptation to deflect compliments will probably be quite strong if it's what you're more comfortable with. But no matter what, try to be patient with yourself. As long as you persevere, eventually you will reach your goal.

Keep in mind that you may not get a lot of compliments on a daily basis. Depending on your social connections, culture, or work/school environment, compliments may or may not be commonplace. Don't let a lack of compliments backfire and reinforce the belief that you don't deserve them. Most people don't get bombarded with compliments every day and may even go several days without getting any positive feedback at all. If you have the same experience, don't be discouraged—this is completely normal. Wait patiently for compliments to come, and take each compliment you get as an opportunity for personal growth.

If you really want to bump up your practice, consider explicitly asking someone you trust to compliment you. You don't have to be secretive about it; you can tell them it's to help you work on your self-esteem. You can even consider providing them with the list of positive traits from chapters 4 and 5 to give them some ideas. If asking someone to compliment you sounds terrifying, keep in mind that the more often you receive and accept compliments, the more quickly you'll habituate to them. Asking a trusted loved one to give you compliments is simply a way to increase your exposure. Don't push yourself too hard, though. There's no reason to completely overwhelm yourself. Find whatever level of discomfort you can manage, and chip away at those defenses by accepting as many compliments as you can.

Stage 2: Believing Compliments

The second stage of responding to compliments goes a little deeper and requires a little more internal work than the first stage, where the focus was on accepting compliments on a purely external basis. Now it's your job to work on accepting compliments *and believing them*. Just like before, it's important to be clear on what believing compliments actually means, because it probably isn't as big of a task as you think.

Believing someone when they compliment you means having faith that they mean what they say. It might be easy to assume that when someone compliments you, they're just being nice, or they're trying to butter you up, or worse—they're patronizing you. At this stage, your job is to trust that none of these things are happening. Here's what it looks like to believe a compliment:

> Person 1: "You did a great job on that presentation."
>
> Person 2: "Thanks. I appreciate the feedback."
>
> Person 2: (thinking to themselves) *Wow, I'm so glad they liked the presentation, even if I didn't think it was good. It was nice of them to tell me that.*

As you can see, this involves an extra step. In addition to your external reaction, believing the intention behind compliments requires you to be a little more mindful of your internal reaction, and to take a minute to acknowledge the difference in opinion. Just like with accepting compliments, this internal piece of believing them can also feel daunting at first. The point of taking this process one step at a time is to make the process more manageable. So to prevent you from making inaccurate assumptions about what this stage is asking of you and feeling overwhelmed as a result, I'll clarify what believing compliments does *not* mean:

- **Believing compliments does not mean you have to agree with the compliments.** You might be in complete disagreement with what the person said, but you don't have to agree in order to believe they might see things differently.
- **Believing compliments does not mean that you assume nobody ever lies.** Yes, some people have ulterior motives when they give compliments, but more often than not, people extend kind words to others

genuinely. Of course, you can practice caution, particularly by identifying people who may have an incentive to give false or exaggerated compliments. However, it's likely that the majority of the people in your life (especially those closest to you) mean what they say when they compliment you.

This stage is all about acknowledging that your self-concept is subjective. If someone sees you in a more positive way than you see yourself, then believing the intention behind their compliment reminds you that you have different opinions. It shows that your negative beliefs about yourself aren't objective facts and they can be changed. If someone else sees you in a positive way, aren't you capable of the same? Keep in mind you don't have to agree with any compliments; you just need to recognize that your self-concept is subjective and it's not a stretch to think of yourself more positively, since others already do. This stage is preparing you for change without forcing it on you.

If you're not sure how to practice believing the intention behind compliments, all you really need to do is make a quick internal acknowledgment of the compliment (for just a few seconds). Here are some things you can say to yourself (internally) when you receive a compliment.

> I don't agree with this compliment, but maybe the other person sees things differently than I do.
>
> They wouldn't have said it if they didn't mean it.
>
> How I see myself isn't a fact, just an opinion.
>
> I'm glad the other person sees me in a positive light.
>
> That was very nice of the other person to say.

Ideally, this reflection would take place immediately after you receive a compliment; however, if compliments are especially uncomfortable, you might be too focused on your discomfort to even remember to believe it. That's okay. Even if you don't remember this step until hours or days after a compliment, you haven't lost your chance. You can still do a quick reflection in hindsight. The timing of the reflection isn't as important as the reflection itself.

By practicing a quick reflection after you receive a compliment, you'll gently call your warped self-concept into question. This will remind you that just because you think something about yourself, that doesn't mean it's true. If other people see you differently than you see yourself, this further highlights the fact that your self-concept is subjective, not factual. And anything that's subjective can be changed under the right circumstances. But don't put too much pressure on yourself. You're not working on actively changing your self-concept at this stage—you're just reminding yourself that your beliefs about yourself aren't set in stone.

Self-Compassion Exercise:
Believing Compliments

Before moving on to the next stage, take some time to focus on this one. Don't start on stage 3 until you've mostly moved past the discomfort of believing the intention behind compliments (again, a 3 or less out of 10 on the discomfort scale). Just like the first stage, this may take some time. In fact, it may take more time to get comfortable believing compliments than it did to get comfortable accepting them: believing is more difficult than accepting, especially when you don't agree with a compliment. It's easy to believe someone when you see things the same way as them! Take as much time as you need to develop a moderate level of habituation, then move on to the third and final stage.

Stage 3: Considering Compliments

This final stage is the deepest and most meaningful for breaking down your defenses, and it requires the most internal work. Let's recap the process so far: first you focused on accepting compliments, then on believing the intention behind them, and now you'll strive to consider whether a compliment might be true. This means taking in the compliment, being open to the *possibility* that the compliment is true, and allowing the compliment to challenge the way you view yourself. The result may include modifying an existing belief about yourself or even adopting a new one, but that's not necessarily required.

This stage of responding to compliments will probably be an ongoing effort that challenges your perception of yourself. No matter how you think of yourself, you'll most likely receive compliments throughout your life that just don't align with your self-concept. When that happens, your instinct should be introspection, not rejection. Right now, your knee-jerk reaction to compliments might be to disagree, but ideally, you should take any compliment you initially disagree with into consideration. Here's what that could look like:

> Person 1: "You did a great job on that presentation."
>
> Person 2: "Thanks. I appreciate the feedback."
>
> Person 2: (thinking to themselves) *Wow, I'm so glad they liked the presentation. I wasn't feeling so good about it, but maybe it was better than I thought.*

In this stage, consider whether the compliment *might* be true by doing a quick internal reflection. It doesn't have to be anything revolutionary. Even 30 seconds of reflection can be pretty impactful, but you're always welcome to reflect for as long as you like.

As we've done with the first two stages, to avoid making inaccurate assumptions of what this stage is asking of you, it's helpful to understand what considering compliments does *not* mean:

- **Considering compliments does not mean you can't form your own opinions.** You don't have to change your mind about how you see yourself every time you get a compliment. It's okay if you don't see yourself exactly how others see you, but you should be open to other perspectives and willing to examine the compliment for accuracy while remembering that the way you see yourself isn't absolute truth and might be inaccurate or unfair.
- **Considering compliments does not mean basing your self-concept on the opinions of others.** If you build your self-esteem on the positive comments you receive from others, you'd develop an unhealthy need for external validation, which isn't an effective way to build your self-esteem since you also allow the negative comments of others to tear you down. Instead, considering compliments is simply a method of challenging your self-concept by being open to possibilities you might not have considered before. Ultimately, you get to make the final call about what's true about you.
- **Considering compliments does not mean you'll become arrogant.** It's okay to think positively of yourself when you receive positive feedback. Being humble doesn't mean resisting praise.

This is the stage where you'll have to actually do something about the cognitive dissonance brought up in the first two stages. In stage 1, you developed a new habit; in stage 2, you acknowledged that your self-concept is subjective and opinions on it can differ; in stage 3, you have to be open to changing your beliefs about yourself when you get positive feedback, which means giving the compliment some consideration before you decide whether to allow it to change your view of yourself or reject it.

Considering compliments may feel like a completely foreign concept to you. If you've never done it before, you may not even be sure how to go about it. If that's the case, here are a few more tips to help you navigate this stage. When you receive a compliment, ask yourself any of these questions:

Is it possible that I'm not assessing myself fairly?

Is there any evidence to support the compliment this person gave me?

Why do I disagree?

Have others given me the same or a similar compliment before?

What would it mean if the person were right?

Your answers to these questions don't matter as much as the fact that you asked them in the first place. There are no right or wrong answers, and sometimes you may not have much of an answer at all! That's okay. What's most important is that you ask the questions with openness and curiosity. Considering compliments doesn't necessarily mean agreeing with them, so even after you ask yourself these questions, you might still decide that the compliment was inaccurate. All you're striving for is remaining open to the perspectives of others and allowing your self-concept to change over time (if necessary) when given new evidence.

Self-Compassion Exercise:

Considering Compliments

For the final self-compassion exercise of this chapter, each time you receive a compliment (and especially if you initially disagree with it), consider whether it could be true. Take a moment to sit with the compliment and allow it to "mingle" with your self-concept. When you feel moderately comfortable considering compliments (you guessed it, a 3 out of 10 on the discomfort scale), then you can move on to the next chapter.

If at the start of this chapter you dreaded compliments because they felt uncomfortable or distressing, hopefully after working through all three stages compliments now feel at worst mundane and at best uplifting. Compliments can be an incredibly powerful tool for rethinking yourself, as long as you use them that way.

Chapter 7

There's Nothing to Be Ashamed Of

Harsh self-criticism is a cornerstone of low self-esteem. It warps your self-concept by magnifying your mistakes and imperfections. Maybe you say things to yourself that are so harsh you'd never say them to someone you care about. You want to be nicer to yourself, but you haven't quite figured out how to shake all those self-critical thoughts. If this is how you feel, I have some good news for you: you've finally reached the point in the book that will teach you how to rethink your self-criticism.

So far, you've addressed your inner critic by reminding yourself that you deserve respect and using cognitive defusion to separate yourself from your inner critic. But these approaches only address the fact that you think critically of yourself, not whether your thoughts are true or accurate. Modifying the content of your self-critical thoughts is an integral step in flattening your fun-house mirror; it helps you take some power back from your inner critic. The next four chapters are all about learning how to rethink your self-criticism. Each chapter will teach you a technique to respond to different types of self-criticism. But don't abandon the techniques you've already learned! They're still important, and you should keep using them when you can. No technique in this book is meant to replace any that came before it—but instead they build off each other.

This chapter addresses a very specific type of self-criticism: the kind that happens in response to a real or perceived moral failing. We're starting here because the concepts you'll learn in this chapter establish a foundational framework that the next three chapters, which cover other types of self-criticism, will build off of. You'll learn that self-criticism isn't always the problem; it's the tone your inner critic uses that makes all the difference. It's not about shutting out your self-critical inner voice; it's about learning how to make it less harsh.

This chapter is dedicated almost entirely to just two emotions: shame and guilt. These emotions are all too familiar to most people with low self-esteem. They're often used interchangeably, but truthfully, there's a world of difference between the two. And knowing the difference can give you a lot of insight into your own self-criticism. By the end of this chapter, you'll be a shame and guilt expert, able to accurately identify these feelings and know what to do when you experience them.

What's the Difference?

To understand the differences between shame and guilt, you first need to understand how they're similar and why they so often get conflated with each other. Both shame and guilt are feelings of remorse or disapproval as a result of some sort of moral or ethical failing. Your intentions don't really matter here; you can experience shame or guilt from your actions even if you meant no harm.

Shame and guilt are emotions, but they're also accompanied by self-critical thoughts. We'll focus on your thoughts in this chapter because that's where self-criticism takes place. Besides, our thoughts are a lot more within our control than our feelings. After all, we can reason with our thoughts. Our emotions? Not so much. Frankly, that's where the similarities end. For two feelings that get lumped together so often, it's surprising how little they actually have in common.

Next, let's address their differences. Three markers of shame help distinguish it from guilt: identification with the misdeed, name-calling, and perception of permanence. But the most important difference is that **guilt, at its core, is a good thing that only needs to be harnessed and managed, while shame, at its core, is never a good thing and must be extinguished.**[1]

Identification with the Misdeed

The most important marker of shame is what it chooses to focus on: you. It equates what you did with who you are. Think of it this way:

> Guilt means "I did a bad thing."
> Shame means "I'm a bad person."

Guilt only focuses on your actions (or inactions), but shame takes it a step further, telling you that your actions define you. When you think about it, that's a really unfair way to evaluate yourself because it leaves no room for mistakes. When you do something bad, it must be because you *are* bad. Each time you mess up, shame further warps your fun-house mirror.

Here's a concrete example. If you told a lie, shame would try to convince you that you must be a liar. It would cause you to harp on about how awful a person you are for telling the lie and transform a single error into an identity. Shame makes it all about you. It's also just not that rational. It really is quite a jump in logic to go from "I told a lie" to "I'm a liar."

On the other hand, guilt focuses on your lie. You would think of the *lie* as disrespectful and deceitful, but you wouldn't think of *yourself* that way. Guilt takes the focus off your character and doesn't call your integrity into question. And not only that, it also allows you to approach those you wronged without centering yourself by indulging in your own perceived character flaws.

Although you should do your best to avoid shame, repeat offenses can make that hard. Sometimes shame feels like a more accurate representation of a situation. For example, if you seem to have a tendency to lie, it's tempting to call yourself a liar because it feels true. While it's not a bad thing to identify a pattern of behavior, it certainly isn't helpful to make that pattern your identity. Just because you struggle with something doesn't mean it should define you.

Name-Calling

It should be no surprise that calling yourself names harms your self-esteem. Name-calling isn't just unnecessarily mean-spirited, but it also reduces your entire personhood down to a single negative trait. And of course, that warps your fun-house mirror by magnifying your misdeeds. Name-calling is also a common component of shame. That's because the goal of shame is to disparage, and sometimes shame can get pretty nasty. For example, when you tell a lie, shame not only causes you to identify with the lie, but it sometimes encourages you to be extra mean to yourself. You might call yourself a "selfish asshole" or a "manipulative bitch."

Guilt, on the other hand, doesn't use name-calling because it's not concerned with who you are as a person. You can feel guilty for something you did without calling yourself names in response. Although name-calling isn't *always* a component of shame, if you catch yourself resorting to name-calling, you can safely bet you're experiencing shame.

Perception of Permanence

Shame is often an overwhelming experience that can make the situation feel unfixable. Instead of focusing on the wrongdoing, which was a fleeting occurrence, shame focuses on your identity, which is permanent. It makes you feel like there's something wrong with you at your core, and that can be a paralyzing feeling. Since shame tries to define who you are, it seems to imply that you'll always behave a certain way. If you label yourself a liar, then you will lie any chance you get. After all, that's what liars do. They lie. Of course, that's just not true or fair.

Some examples of shame thoughts that imply permanence are "I fail at everything," "I can't do anything right," or "I'm broken." These are pretty hopeless thoughts to have. By comparison, guilt focuses on a single misdeed, which can often be rectified (I'll get to that part later in the chapter), so it doesn't feel quite so hopeless. In fact, guilt represents your desire to do better. Shame, on the other hand, concludes that you're not even capable of good.

When you feel like something in you is broken beyond repair, it seems like the most reasonable thing to do is give up. In fact, there's considerable evidence that shame has a de-motivating effect,[2] even though people often think they can use it to whip themselves into shape. It's a lot easier to rectify a single misdeed than to change who you are as a person. So when you're faced with regret, ask yourself, Am I compelled to right a wrong, or am I paralyzed by the sense of hopelessness that nothing will change?

Guilt vs. Empathy

Just as it's important to understand the difference between guilt and shame, it's also important to understand the difference between guilt and empathy. It may not seem like it at first, but guilt and empathy often get mistaken for each other, which can be a major source of unnecessary self-criticism.

Let's start with their similarities. Both guilt and empathy are negative emotional experiences. Even though we think of empathy as a positive thing, most of the time when we feel it, it doesn't exactly feel good. You might feel empathy when someone you know loses their job, or when a tornado wipes out someone else's house, or when someone is being mistreated. All these situations are painful, which means that empathy can also be a very painful experience. Guilt and empathy feel similar because they're both negative emotional experiences in reaction to something that went wrong.

The difference between guilt and empathy comes down to responsibility. When you experience empathy, you assume no personal responsibility for the other person's hardship. You simply feel bad for the other person, and that's it. Empathy stops there. But when you experience guilt, you take it a step further by taking the blame. In situations when you're actually at fault, guilt is an appropriate reaction. But people with low self-esteem sometimes instinctually blame themselves by taking responsibility for someone else's negative feelings when they did nothing to cause them.

Empathy means "I feel bad for that person."
Guilt means "I feel bad for that person and it's my fault."

Taming self-criticism doesn't always mean being kind to yourself when you do something wrong. Sometimes it means not allowing yourself to take responsibility for things you didn't actually do. Here's an example. Imagine waking up one morning with a fever and having to call in sick, to take care of yourself but also to ensure you don't get anyone else sick. However, if you don't go to work, your team will be short-staffed, which will subject them to added stress. Your instinct might be to feel guilty, because on the surface it seems like you're the cause of their added stress. But you didn't actually do anything wrong, and by feeling guilty you're just taking on responsibility that isn't yours. Instead, empathy is a more appropriate reaction. Empathy allows you to acknowledge and empathize with the stress on your team *without accepting blame for it.*

Letting go of unnecessary blame will get easier with practice, but it's important that you remind yourself that even if you *feel* guilty, it's not always as appropriate for the situation as empathy. Sometimes you can't reasonably blame yourself, but you can still feel negatively about the consequences of an unfortunate situation, just without unnecessary self-blame.

Letting Go of Shame

Now that you know why shame is so damaging to your self-esteem, the next step is learning to let it go. That doesn't simply mean justifying or ignoring your misdeeds; when you do something wrong, it's appropriate to feel some remorse and even some self-criticism. Letting go of shame after you've done something wrong just involves replacing your shame with guilt. That's because guilt is healthier and much easier to manage than shame, and it's usually a form of legitimate self-criticism, whereas shame is just harsh self-criticism. Legitimate self-criticism, as you recall, isn't something you should shy away from, even if it's uncomfortable. But harsh self-criticism is detrimental to your self-esteem.

Guiding your thoughts toward guilt instead of shame might go against your instincts at first. Before you started this book, you might have believed that all self-criticism is bad and therefore assumed that the goal is to eliminate your self-criticism entirely. The truth is, self-criticism that's constructive and holds you accountable to your values is good, so getting rid of that type of self-criticism would be disastrous.

Developing a nuanced approach to your self-criticism will be difficult, and it'll take some practice. Just be patient with yourself and work through the steps at your own pace. Building your self-esteem is a process and certainly not a race!

Is It Shame?

You can't let go of shame unless you can identify it accurately. So when you experience remorse for a misdeed, your first step is to carefully determine whether it's shame or guilt. Keep in mind that you might be feeling a little of both. That's okay; your thoughts and feelings don't always have to fit neatly into a singular category. Taking what you learned earlier in the chapter, look for these markers of shame:

Identification with the misdeed
Name-calling
Perception of permanence

Here are some questions you can ask yourself to identify these factors:

> Am I focusing on *myself* or *what I did*?
>
> Am I calling myself names?
>
> Am I feeling completely hopeless and unmotivated or even unable to make things better?

At the same time, look out for any indication that empathy is actually more appropriate for the situation than shame or guilt. To do that, ask yourself, Have I actually done anything wrong? If not, you can stop here. Remind yourself that you can empathize with someone else's distress or hardship without taking the blame for it. You don't need to respond to your inner critic when there's nothing to criticize.

You might also sometimes experience unnecessary guilt about things that aren't moral issues, like what you choose to eat or how messy your home is. You haven't done anything morally wrong, so guilt isn't an appropriate reaction. That doesn't necessarily mean you shouldn't care about those things, but you should be mindful about where you attach morals to non-moral issues. These types of self-criticism will be addressed in the next chapter.

Reframe Your Thoughts to Eradicate Shame

If you've identified even a speck of shame in your thoughts, you'll need to modify your thinking to rid yourself of shame-based self-talk. Even if you're experiencing shame and guilt at the same time, you have to let go of the shame before you can address the guilt. While guilt can be harnessed into a positive action (more on that in a bit), shame is an impediment to progress. Trying to work through guilt without first eradicating shame is like trying to empty the water out of a sinking boat without repairing the hole that's taking on water.

To eradicate shame, you need to modify the way you think about the situation. Now this part might sound weird: **the goal is not to make your thoughts more positive.** A common misconception about managing your inner critic is that you're supposed to turn a negative thought into a positive one. But if you've committed some sort of misdeed, it would be a disservice to everyone involved if you tried to make it into a positive thing. You have to be able to take accountability for what you did, but in a way that doesn't damage your self-esteem. Shame is always detrimental to self-esteem, but guilt doesn't have to be. The problem with shame isn't that it's negative, it's that the negativity is focused on the wrong thing (you).

The most effective way to reframe shame-based thinking is to make the thoughts resemble guilt instead. Since shame and guilt have some similarities, reframing your thinking from shame to guilt is a much smaller and more realistic shift than reframing your thinking from shame to peace, for example. Once your thoughts more closely resemble guilt, you can channel that guilt into positive action. Until then, there's nothing productive you can do with shame.

Here are examples of how to modify your thinking by avoiding the markers of shame:

Identification with the Misdeed

Once you've identified a shame-based thought, ask yourself if you're focusing more on yourself or what you did. If your thoughts are more about yourself, then try to direct your attention to what you did wrong instead. Focus on what you didn't like about your actions, not what you don't like about yourself. Here are some examples:

> I'm a bad person → I did a bad thing
>
> I'm a liar → I told a lie

Remember: you're not trying to turn a negative into a positive. The modified thought is still negative, and it still doesn't feel good to acknowledge. The difference is that the thought doesn't attack your character. Once you're able to focus on what you did rather than who you are, you can take steps to rectify your actions.

Even after modifying your thought, it can be difficult to let go of that nagging question: *What if I'm actually just a bad person?* People with low self-esteem are often very preoccupied with whether or not they're a good person. Funnily enough, being preoccupied with the strength of your character is more a sign of integrity. That's because in order to be a good person, you have to be willing to examine and question yourself at times. Instead of legitimizing the worry that you might be bad, you should let the question itself remind you that you care about being good.

Name-Calling

Shame doesn't always involve name-calling, but when you notice that you're calling yourself nasty names, you can safely bet you're experiencing shame. Try to be specific about what action or inaction caused you to call yourself a name and describe what happened without insulting yourself. Here are some examples:

> I'm such an idiot → I can't believe I did that
>
> I'm useless trash → I'm not proud of my actions

Perception of Permanence

Shame causes you to make unfair or exaggerated conclusions about your misdeed. Do you feel completely hopeless that anything can ever get better? If so, there's a high chance you're experiencing shame. Make sure to keep your focus on the current problem instead of reminding yourself of similar things you've done in the past. Don't compile a list of evidence against yourself; that's distracting and unhelpful. Here are some examples of how to reframe your thoughts:

> I'll never be good at this → I messed this one up
>
> I fail at everything → I failed at this

Even if you notice a pattern of the same misdeed happening over and over, remind yourself that shame isn't a helpful way to think about the problem. It doesn't promote accountability or change; it just promotes self-deprecation. If you notice a negative character trait, keep it in mind for chapter 11, where you'll learn how to rethink your weaknesses. But for now, it's important to try to focus on a single issue at a time.

Be Patient and Trust the Process

This shame-and-guilt framework makes logical sense, and it's a concept that most people can grasp on a rational level. But in practice, it might feel forced or insincere at first. That's because while your brain might be on board with the idea, your gut may not be. When there's a disconnect between your logical thoughts and your deeper beliefs, the bridge between the two is really just repeated exposure. It takes time for you to get enough familiarity with a new idea in order for it to feel normal to you.

Think of it this way: all of your best friends were once strangers. When you were just getting to know them, you didn't have enough comfort or familiarity to feel a deep sense of connection with them. But over time and with repeated interactions, you built an intimate relationship that now feels meaningful. The same will happen with your thoughts. New thought patterns might feel very unfamiliar right now, but if you continue to engage with them over time, they'll feel a lot more genuine. Time is key!

Managing Guilt

Many people with low self-esteem use self-deprecation as their go-to guilt-management strategy. They believe their inner critic can alleviate them of their guilt by berating them as a form of penance. When a client articulates this to me, I make a point to ask, "How's that been working for you?" And the answer is always "Not great." That's because most likely what they're really doing is shaming themselves, which is more effective at making them feel worthless than absolving their guilt. Even when it seems like you "deserve" punishment via self-deprecation, at the end of it, you'll probably find that it didn't do much good. The cleansing you thought you'd experience through punishment was nothing more than an illusion.

There's a better way to manage guilt, and it involves a few steps. The first step, admittedly, is optional, but it can be incredibly impactful, particularly when you have low self-esteem. Start by seeking understanding about what the guilt really means. If you're not careful, you might inadvertently allow guilt to serve as a personal indictment. After all, guilt is a negative emotion, and it's easy to equate a negative feeling with a negative state of being. Good people don't feel this way, right?

To understand what guilt means, it's helpful to first consider what the absence of guilt would mean. Since we often don't realize the value of something until it's gone, this can be quite an illuminating thought experiment. Take this example: Imagine you insulted your partner during the heat of an argument and you feel terrible about it after the fact. We'll assume you've already reframed your thoughts to eliminate shame and now all you're left with is guilt. You recognize that what you did was wrong, but you can't let it go. That's a pretty typical reaction to the situation. But now imagine you did the same thing, *except you don't feel guilty about it*. What would that mean? It may mean that you don't value kindness, respect, or even your partner very much. In this example, it's easy to see that the absence of guilt is more of a personal indictment than the presence of it. Guilt isn't a sign that you're bad—actually, it's often the opposite.

In fact, guilt is your moral compass. It's what keeps you accountable to your values.

The more strongly you value something, the more guilty you feel when you do something that goes against your values; the guilt you feel is a reminder of your values. It's confirmation that you're above your wrongdoing, because if you weren't, the wrongdoing wouldn't be embarrassing or dishonorable. It's okay to feel guilt from time to time. The only way to be truly immune to it is to not have values or morals at all.

It's weird at first to think about how such an awful, insufferable emotion can be evidence of a strong moral character. That's why I usually get a puzzled look when I respond to my client's expression of guilt by saying, "I'm really glad you feel guilty about that." Because, in fact, I'd be quite worried about a person who doesn't feel guilty after they do something wrong. We all mess up sometimes. We've all got regrets. That shouldn't determine whether we're good or bad. What we should try to focus on instead is our capacity for feeling guilt when we mess up and our desire to atone for that guilt. So when you feel guilty for something you did, try to think of it this way:

I'm a [positive attribute] who sometimes [negative action].

For example:

> I'm a good person who sometimes does bad things.
>
> I'm an honest person who sometimes lies.
>
> I'm a generous person who sometimes acts out of self-interest.

Framing your thoughts like this demonstrates that a single misstep doesn't undo all your other positive qualities. It helps you zoom out and recognize that who you are is so much bigger than just one action, that good people sometimes do bad things. At the same time, it doesn't minimize or ignore what you did. Disregarding all of your poor decisions isn't the right way to build your self-esteem. You have to do a bit of a balancing act between accepting and allowing productive feelings of guilt (when necessary) while avoiding shame, which warps your self-concept.

You should only do this step when it feels (at least mostly) believable that one misstep doesn't make you a bad person. Lying to yourself will do you no good. There's no need to force a different perspective on yourself. Every situation is unique, and this method might work for some situations and not others. Use your discretion.

While this first step in the process is a nice way to think about guilt, it doesn't do anything to absolve you of it. That's why it's an optional step. The next step (atonement) has a more practical objective.

Atonement

Guilt, like many other emotions, demands action. It's an incredibly compelling emotion. When we feel guilty, we want to do whatever it takes to absolve ourselves of it. This is good news for guilt management, because it means there are actionable steps you can take to reduce the guilt you feel. But remember, punishment in the form of relentless harsh self-criticism is not atonement. It may feel tempting, like you "deserve" it, but it probably won't be as effective as it initially seems.

There are essentially two methods to atone for a misdeed: moving backward or moving forward. Moving backward involves reversing or fixing whatever action or inaction caused the guilt in the first place. For example, imagine that your friend is sick and asks you to pick up a few things for them at the drugstore. When you get to their house, you realize that you forgot one of the items they needed and you feel guilty for your mistake. You can move backward from this misdeed by going back to the drugstore and purchasing the item you forgot. The only harm done is that your friend had to wait a little longer for that item, but at least you fulfilled your promise to them and they got what they needed. You've done what your guilt compelled you to do; your guilt fulfilled its purpose and you no longer need it. You have atoned.

Unfortunately, moving backward is only a viable option in a small number of situations. For most misdeeds, the damage has already been done and there's nothing you can do to reverse it. In these situations, it's easy to get stuck. When moving backward and fixing the mistake isn't possible, you might experience the hopeless feeling that you'll never be able to live it down. But this is when you should instead focus on moving forward.

Moving forward is the alternative method of atonement when moving backward isn't possible. It involves taking steps to prevent future misdeeds, accommodating anyone who was hurt or inconvenienced, and of course apologizing. For example, imagine that you've canceled plans with your family to go to a concert with your friend. You highly value your family and you impacted their plans, so you feel horrible about your actions in hindsight. You can't go back in time and choose your family over the concert, so your only choice is to make sure you don't make the same mistake again. You can even go the extra mile by buying your family a nice dinner to make up for the impact you had on their plans. At least this way you're making an effort to bring something positive to the situation. It doesn't fix the problem, but it offsets a bad deed with a good one.

Apologizing Only When Necessary

Apologies are often an essential component of atonement. But sometimes apologies aren't necessary, and apologizing *too much* can actually harm your self-esteem. Think about it: if you're constantly apologizing, wouldn't you start to feel like a burden or a failure?

An important part of atoning for your misdeeds without harming your self-esteem is determining when apologizing is necessary. To do that, you need to identify the purpose of your apology. Although it might sound counterintuitive at first, you might sometimes apologize to prioritize your own feelings over the feelings of the person you're apologizing to. When an apology is self-serving, it can have more of a negative impact on your self-esteem than a positive one.

There are three ways an apology can be self-serving.

Reassurance-seeking in disguise. The first way an apology can be self-serving is when it's really reassurance-seeking disguised as an apology. An apology can sometimes just be a sneaky bid for information about how the other person feels. Hearing them say "Oh don't worry about it, it didn't bother me" is a huge relief and benefits you more than the person you apologized to. If that's one of your reasons for apologizing, it isn't very sincere. It's just a way to reassure yourself that everything is okay. Aside from being less sincere, when you rely too much on reassurance, it eventually erodes your ability to trust your own judgment. When you seek reassurance, you default to the assumption that you did something wrong unless told otherwise. That's a dangerous habit to fall into, and assuming wrongdoing by default is disastrous for your self-esteem.

Protection from criticism. The second way an apology can be self-serving is when it's meant to protect you from external criticism. This happens when you tack a self-deprecating statement onto your apology ("I'm sorry, I know I can be annoying sometimes"). While it may sound counterproductive at first, this type of apology is a strategy to prevent others from criticizing you too harshly by beating them to the punch. It's a protective measure in the short-term, but it can be destructive to your self-esteem over time. Not to mention, these apologies also aren't sincere since their purpose is to protect you from criticism from others, not to make amends.

Absolving yourself of guilt. The third and final way an apology can be self-serving is when your intention for apologizing is to absolve yourself of guilt. Apologizing excessively is an attempt to (often fruitlessly) force guilt out of your conscience. The problem is that by doing this you're shifting the burden onto the person you're apologizing to. After the fifteenth apology, they might start to feel compelled to offer comfort by minimizing their own feelings. ("Don't worry about it, it wasn't that big of a deal.") And as a result, the apology becomes more about rectifying *your* feelings than those of the person you're apologizing to.

When you've truly done something wrong and an apology is owed, you should certainly apologize. But if you get the sense that apologizing would serve your own needs rather than the person you're apologizing to, you may want to reconsider. Here are three tips for offering sincere, effective, and empathetic apologies:

Try saying "thank you." Saying "thank you" is not only a less self-centered way to apologize, but it's also a lot more positive. Instead of saying, "I'm sorry I'm late," try "Thank you for waiting for me." By thanking the other person, you're not only avoiding unnecessary self-criticism, but you're also focusing on the appreciation you have *for the other person*. It typically feels a lot better on the receiving end because it's nice to feel appreciated.

This technique is helpful, but it has limits. By no means should you eliminate the word "sorry" from your vocabulary in favor of "thank you." Replacing an apology with gratitude is generally more appropriate for relatively minor slights. For larger offenses, a standard apology is almost always more appropriate.

Focus on the other person. To avoid a self-serving apology, simply focus on the other person instead. For example, a self-serving apology might sound like "I'm sorry, I'm so annoying." As you can see, it's all about you. You're at the center of this apology, and there's no mention of the other person's feelings or hardship. Instead, focus on the other person by acknowledging how your actions impacted them. For example, "I'm sorry, you shouldn't have had to deal with that." This apology not only curbs unnecessary self-criticism but also shows empathy, which the self-serving apology lacks.

Don't dwell on the apology. It's really uncomfortable to sit with the feeling that you've upset or inconvenienced another person. The urge to smother them with apologies to rid yourself of the overwhelming guilt is palpable. But that's self-serving, because more than one apology truly doesn't go very far for the person you're apologizing to. While it's nice to hear an apology when we've been slighted in some way, the second, third, fourth, and fifteenth apologies really don't offer anything more than the first one. It's best to keep it simple by just saying it once. Show genuine remorse, empathy, and a commitment to make it better somehow, then move on.

Residual Guilt

While these guilt-management strategies are helpful, they're certainly not a silver bullet. In some situations, there's a good chance that even after going through all these steps, you'll still feel a little bit guilty. That's okay. Even if you can change the way you think about the situation, you might still struggle to move on from guilt on a deeper, more emotional level. Feelings aren't as quick to adopt new ideas as thoughts are. You might have experienced this during a breakup, for example, when your thoughts told you that you needed the split but your feelings said otherwise. If you're struggling with this cognitive dissonance, give your feelings a little patience. They just need some time to catch up with your thoughts.

While atonement can help alleviate some guilt, perhaps nothing is as effective as time. If you're still experiencing residual guilt even after trying everything you can think of, grant yourself the patience to sit in that emotion until it passes on its own. Hopefully by connecting with the meaning of guilt (that guilt signifies your values), the guilt will be a little more tolerable, and you can be more willing to sit with it.

It's also important to consider, given the individual circumstances of the misdeed, how realistic it is to expect the guilt to just go away altogether. For some misdeeds, all the time in the world still might not be enough to exoner-ate you from the guilt you feel in response. You might look back on a certain action years from now and still feel a tinge of remorse. Time might help the feeling fade, but the stain may never leave. This is a realistic, albeit painful, expectation to have. In fact, being completely absolved from past guilts might inadvertently lead you to make the same mistakes again. It's easy to think that we can't move on from guilt until it's completely gone, but this sentiment isn't entirely helpful. In fact, it might actually be a good thing to look back on past wrongs and still feel a little guilt. It's probably only possible to completely let go of guilt by a) forgetting about the misdeed altogether or b) changing your values. Often the key to guilt management is not to abolish the guilt but to move on from it.

Self-Compassion Exercise:
Letting Go of Shame and Managing Guilt

Now it's your turn to put everything you learned in this chapter to use. Don't expect to be perfect at it right off the bat, though. Shame can be such a dis-orienting negative emotion that you might have a hard time accessing logical thinking and critical awareness. Even if you know what to do in response to shame, it's easy to feel like that knowledge is completely inaccessible because it's been so violently eclipsed by the emotional experience of it all.

If you feel that using these techniques in the moment just isn't possible for you, start by building your familiarity with them in retrospect. In fact, retro-spect can shed more light on a situation. Say you've just come out of a shame spiral. The dust is starting to settle and you recognize that the thoughts you were having were neither kind nor helpful. While you can't go back in time and change your thoughts, you can learn from them. Work through the exercise as soon as you're able to recognize the shame. Even if the shame spiral was three days ago and the feeling has already passed, get acquainted with the process as soon as you're able. Build some mental muscle memory. The more regularly you do so, the easier the exercise will feel when you really do need it.

In an ideal world, you'd be able to put all of this into practice in the very moments you experience shame. But we don't live in an ideal world. You don't have to start at the desired end result; you just have to start *somewhere*. And for right now, a completely acceptable *somewhere* to start is in retrospect.

On the next page is a step-by-step guide to help you let go of your shame and manage your guilt. When you experience shame or guilt, use this guide to help you practice each step in the process.

To download a free copy of this worksheet, visit rethinkyourself.info/worksheets or scan the QR code in the back of the book.

Situation:

_____

_____

Shame-based thought:

_____

Which markers of shame were present? Circle all that apply:

Identification with   Name-Calling   Perception
the Misdeed   of Permanence

Reframed thought:

_____

Personal values that were violated:

_____

Optional: I'm a _____

who sometimes _____

Atonement: How can you make amends (moving forward or backward)?

_____

_____

Chapter 8

~~~

Your Inner Critic—Friend or Foe?

You know your inner critic well. It makes daily unwanted appearances in your thoughts and constantly torments you by reminding you that you're not "good enough." You probably want more than anything for it to just go away. And maybe you're hoping this book will teach you how to do that. The inconvenient truth is that you can't just make your inner critic go away. And more importantly, you shouldn't do that even if it were possible. Your inner critic isn't supposed to be your enemy, even if it feels like one right now.

When you have low self-esteem, you can't help but think of your inner critic as your enemy. It seems to always find something wrong with you, insulting you relentlessly day in and day out, so it's a big reason your fun-house mirror is so warped. Maybe your inner critic has even gotten in the way of the self-compassion exercises in previous chapters. It may have told you that you don't deserve to feel good about yourself, or that it's impossible because you're a bad person, or that you're doing everything wrong. If you want to be kinder to yourself, the answer isn't to silence, ignore, or "beat" your inner critic. As difficult as it may sound, the most effective approach is to learn how to work *with* your inner critic rather than *against* it.

This chapter will teach you how to rethink another type of self-criticism. So far, you've learned how to respond to the moral type of self-criticism. But not all self-criticism involves your morals. Sometimes you might feel self-critical for getting a bad grade on an exam, or making a joke that doesn't quite land, or procrastinating on a project. These aren't moral issues, so the shame-and-guilt approach doesn't really work that well. You'll learn a new approach to add to your toolkit as you continue to flatten your warped fun-house mirror. This approach won't involve ignoring your imperfections, but instead allowing them to exist in your self-concept without overmagnifying them.

This chapter will focus on the type of self-criticism that attacks your skills, attributes, habits, or personality. For many, this type of self-criticism is both the most frequent and the most stubborn. It's the feeling that, even despite your best efforts, you just aren't good enough. You'll never do anything right, nobody likes you, you're a loser . . . the list can go on and on, but you get the idea.

The good news is that taming this type of self-criticism is quite similar to the shame-and-guilt approach, just with a few minor adjustments. It starts with *unlearning* something you think you know about self-criticism: that self-criticism and self-compassion are not opposites.

The Self-Compassion Myth

To think of self-criticism as anything but the opposite of self-compassion probably sounds a bit misguided. But hear me out. Having self-esteem isn't about ignoring your shortcomings. That's arrogance. No matter where your self-esteem is, you're going to experience self-criticism from time to time, and that's okay. Self-criticism isn't an inherently bad thing. The fact that you could improve on things doesn't mean you aren't good enough. It just means that growth is a lifelong process. People with a strong self-esteem are able to bridge the gap between self-compassion and self-criticism. They're able to criticize themselves *but do it with compassion*. And if you want to have a strong self-esteem, you'll need to learn how to do that too.

Think of self-compassion and self-criticism like a Venn diagram. Right now, you (like most people) probably think that self-criticism and self-compassion are mutually exclusive and completely separate concepts, like the two circles below. They seem to share nothing in common. There is no overlap.

Self-criticism   *Self-compassion*

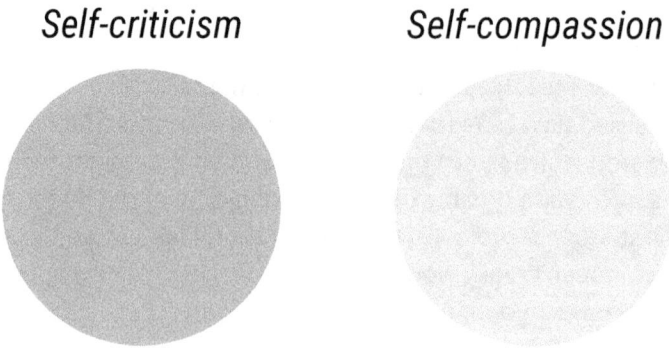

Intuitively, self-compassion just seems like the absence of self-criticism. So if you want to be self-compassionate, you might assume the best way to do that is by somehow silencing your inner critic. After all, most people would agree that self-criticism is a bad thing. But when we think of self-criticism like this, we end up trying to prove our inner critic wrong or just learning how to ignore it. And while that approach makes sense at face value, there are a few problems with it. Most importantly, this approach just doesn't work. If it did, none of us would have any issues with self-criticism. We'd recite a few affirmations and be good to go. The reason this approach usually doesn't work is that there's usually a little bit (or sometimes a lot) of truth behind your self-criticism. When you try to convince yourself otherwise, it just feels like you're lying to yourself. And lies just aren't convincing. But aside from this approach not being that effective, it's also not healthy. As uncomfortable as our inner critic makes us feel sometimes, we need it.

Let's do a quick thought experiment. Imagine that you wake up and your inner critic is gone forever. You've completely lost the ability to recognize your limitations or think critically about your actions. At first, you might feel a sense of relief. That pesky inner voice has left you alone for good. You might feel lighter and more free.

But if you think about this scenario in a little more detail, it becomes clear that it would create quite a few problems as well. You'd be pompous, unwilling to ever admit personal wrongdoing. You wouldn't be accountable to your word because you'd never feel bad if you broke it. You'd lose all awareness of the areas of yourself that need growth. Truthfully, you'd be even worse off in life without an inner critic than you are with an overly harsh one.

What this thought experiment demonstrates is that your inner critic isn't the problem. In fact, as odd as it may seem, having an inner critic is actually a good thing! But it's only helpful when you've got a good working partnership with it. So the real goal of inner-critic management isn't to silence your inner critic, but instead to teach it how to be more compassionate. Sounds absolutely backwards, right? Just stick with me.

It's not helpful to assume that self-criticism and self-compassion are mutually exclusive concepts. In fact, there's a lot of overlap between the two. And where they intersect is where self-esteem flourishes. Let's take a closer look at each segment of the Venn diagram to understand why that's the case.

Self-criticism   *Self-compassion*

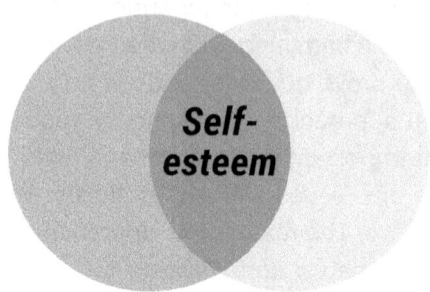

Self-esteem

The first segment in the Venn diagram, pure self-criticism, is probably pretty familiar to you. It's harsh, cruel, and miserable and obviously isn't healthy at all. But the reason it's unhealthy isn't because of the presence of self-criticism; it's because of the absence of self-compassion. It's an extreme, and as you'll see, the other extreme isn't so healthy either.

The third segment, pure self-compassion, is what I describe as "indulgent self-compassion." It's about only doing what feels good (like ignoring your mistakes) rather than what's healthy (like being accountable to them). It's completely devoid of self-discipline and even self-awareness. Although it feels great in small doses, kindness without discipline isn't self-compassion; it's unhealthy self-indulgence. As you saw with the thought experiment earlier, if you lacked the capacity to be self-critical, you'd get yourself into a lot of trouble. That's not really something to aim for. Instead, you've got to embrace a little bit of healthy self-criticism, which involves making the difficult choice to face the pain of self-criticism rather than deny it or explain it away. To do that, you need to teach your inner critic how to deliver criticism with compassion.

That brings us to the middle segment, where self-criticism and self-compassion overlap. When you exist here, you hold yourself accountable to your values and you have the necessary awareness of your growth edges. It's exceptionally difficult to achieve personal growth if you're unable to think critically about yourself. Your inner critic keeps you accountable by pushing you to do things that you don't like doing, simply because they're good for you. Existing in this overlap also helps you balance confidence with humility and keeps your ego from inflating too far. Self-criticism never feels good, but that doesn't mean it's bad. Sometimes you need your inner critic to keep you in check. It's not all sunshine and rainbows, but it's exactly where genuine self-esteem lives.

The reality is that we all have shortcomings, and we all make mistakes. No one is immune to criticism, but that doesn't mean we deserve to be insulted and disrespected every time we mess up. As backward as it sounds, self-criticism can be compassionate. It's not an oxymoron. Self-esteem isn't the absence of self-criticism. In other words, you don't achieve a healthy self-esteem by ignoring your weaknesses; you do it by acknowledging them with fairness and kindness. If you start to pay attention to your inner critic rather than immediately reacting to it with defensiveness, you might find that it's actually invested in your growth and self-discipline.

The Purpose of Your Inner Critic

Your inner critic has a legitimate purpose, and it's not just to torture you, I promise. When it operates the way it's supposed to, your inner critic can actually be incredibly helpful, but when you treat it like an enemy, it can't offer you any assistance.

When we criticize ourselves, it often feels nothing short of destructive. But in interpersonal contexts, it's a lot easier to acknowledge that sometimes criticism can be constructive. Constructive criticism, when delivered compassionately, promotes accountability, growth, and self-discipline. However, you can't have any of those things without the ability to think critically of yourself when you fall out of line. But because self-criticism can be so painful, it's easy to lose sight of its benefits, which ends up getting a lot of people stuck in an endless loop of pushing away their inner critics, which just end up pushing right back.

Have you ever watched a really bad TV talent show audition and thought, *Why did their loved ones allow them to come on this show and embarrass themselves?* If their loved ones had given them a little bit of constructive feedback, the person might have been spared the embarrassment of believing their audition was better than it actually was. In the end, the lack of critical feedback didn't serve them well. In fact, it would have been more compassionate for their loved ones to hurt their feelings with gentle truths than allow them to remain blind to their limitations and ultimately embarrass themselves publicly. That's because criticism isn't always bad! We often conflate criticism with disrespect. Of course, there's sometimes overlap between the two, but criticism is not always disrespectful. When it's true and constructive, self-criticism is actually more compassionate than lies that make us feel good.

It's easy to acknowledge the benefits of constructive criticism. But for some reason, when we criticize ourselves, that idea gets lost. For example, imagine that you've noticed that you've been doing a lot of online impulse shopping lately. Not only has this wrecked your budget, but it also feels wasteful and materialistic. It feels like a problem of your own doing, and you can't help but criticize yourself for it. You want to ignore the pain of self-criticism, but you just can't shake it. Your inner critic attacks you relentlessly, calling you careless and irresponsible. It feels like your inner critic is completely against you.

Now, imagine the same scenario but without any self-criticism. You don't really care much that your finances are a mess. After all, you deserve a little treat now and then. Self-compassion means doing whatever makes you feel good, right? Ironically, if this were your attitude about self-criticism, it would mean you don't care that much about doing what's best for you (and the world). You're allowing a bad habit to continue unmitigated because you're unable to think critically of your own actions. In this example, having no self-criticism is actually worse than having harsh self-criticism!

The ability to think critically of your actions helps you identify problems and formulate solutions. Maybe the reason you're buying so many things you don't need is because you think they'll make you happy or give you status. Instead, you could be more disciplined with your spending, which would take some effort but surely pay off in the long run. Without your inner critic, you'd never reach this realization. When you look at it this way, it's easy to see that your inner critic serves a pretty important purpose. Right now, it may not always be effective at fulfilling that purpose, but that's where you come in, to teach it how to be more compassionate. And the first step is to stop arguing with it.

Don't Argue with Your Inner Critic

At first, it seems counterintuitive to resist arguing with your inner critic. That approach may be at odds with how you've approached self-criticism until now. It's also a little scary to imagine what could happen if you stopped fighting your inner critic. What will it get away with if you don't keep it in check? But fighting your inner critic doesn't stop it from criticizing you.

Think of it this way: if someone insults you, are they going to suddenly give you the compassion you deserve because you showed them who's boss? Compassion isn't granted as a concession. If you're mean to your inner critic, why would it be nice to you in response? Chances are you've tried this before and you know it doesn't work. Every time you push away your inner critic, it pushes right back. Not only is picking a fight with your inner critic ineffective, but it also restricts your self-esteem development. Here are a few reasons for that:

Sometimes Your Inner Critic Is Right

Everyone has weaknesses and everyone makes mistakes. You don't need to transform every negative thought you have into a positive one—sometimes there just isn't a way to put a positive spin on a situation. Sometimes the truth is that you just aren't so good at something or you've made a genuine error, and there's no way around it. Just because your self-criticism was painful doesn't mean it was wrong. It's okay if you mess up or simply have a weakness. That doesn't give you the right to insult or demean yourself.

A common tactic the inner critic uses is the word "more."

> "You could be exercising *more*."
>
> "You could be spending *more* time with your kids."
>
> "You could be working *more*."
>
> "You could reach out to your friends *more*."

And technically, your inner critic is right about all of those things. No matter how much you're doing, it's always possible to do *more*. This type of criticism sets you up to fail because *more* is not a measurement. More is like infinity: it never ends. When *more* is the goal, you'll never achieve it. Just because you could be doing *more* doesn't mean you aren't doing *enough*. In this case, like many others, your inner critic is right; you certainly could be doing more. Luckily, your inner critic doesn't have to be wrong for you to do something about it. You can give up the battle of right vs. wrong—it simply isn't the point.

Your Counterarguments Probably Won't Be Convincing

Sometimes my clients tell me that they try to counteract their self-critical thoughts with positive thoughts. My first question when they tell me this is, Do you believe those positive thoughts more than the self-critical ones? Usually the answer is no. That's because there's usually some element of truth in our self-criticism, and it's hard to prove something wrong when it seems so true.

Force-feeding yourself affirmations in response to your self-criticism only works when the affirmations are more convincing than the self-criticism. Most of the time, they just aren't—but not because the affirmations aren't true. It's more likely that you're not open to accepting them. It's really hard to make a 180-degree change from self-criticism to self-praise. Our brains usually can't handle that drastic of a perspective shift. A more middle-ground approach is usually a lot more effective.

Arguing with Your Inner Critic Promotes Perfectionism

The instinct to argue with your inner critic is understandable. Self-criticism is a painful experience, and I can't fault anyone for wanting to avoid it. But a defensive response to self-criticism is rooted in the false belief that being "good enough" means being exempt from criticism. The problem is that the only way to be truly exempt from criticism is to be perfect; since nobody can be perfect, the next best thing is to pretend you are.

Unfortunately, this is how self-esteem is often portrayed. But when you're so threatened by criticism that you feel the need to deny your shortcomings, you don't have a strong self-esteem. People with strong self-esteem can face criticism, even though it's painful. They have the ability to weigh their self-criticism and grow from it if they need to. Self-criticism isn't the enemy of a strong self-esteem. When you treat it like it is, you uphold the lie that you're only good enough when your inner critic has nothing to criticize.

Mutual Validation:
The Bridge to Compassionate Self-Criticism

If you indiscriminately silence your inner critic, you'll lose out on the benefits your legitimate self-criticism has to offer. Most of the time, even your harsh self-criticism has a little bit of truth behind it. The problem is that your inner critic too often conveys legitimate criticism using exaggerations and insults. So to make your inner critic more compassionate, rather than teaching it how to be less critical, you need to teach it how to deliver critical feedback more compassionately, and hold it accountable when it doesn't. To do that, you'll use a technique called mutual validation.

Mutual validation comes from an assertiveness technique used for interpersonal communication, but you can apply the same principles to your self-criticism. This technique is a way to respond to opposition without attacking the opposing party. It involves validating both perspectives rather than pitting them against each other. For example, if you like romantic comedies and someone else doesn't, you can validate both points by saying, "I understand why you think rom-coms are cheesy; I find them kind of comforting and light-hearted, even if they are a little cheesy sometimes." Just because you disagree doesn't mean one person is right and the other is wrong. You can express your thoughts while also seeing the validity in the other person's perspective.

It gets a little trickier when part, but not all, of another person's perspective is valid. For example, if a friend makes fun of your taste in music, their difference in musical preference is valid but their disrespectful words are not. You might use mutual validation by saying, "It's okay if you have a different taste in music. I happen to like this genre of music, so please don't make fun of it." In this example, instead of responding aggressively, you chose to simply highlight two conflicting viewpoints as valid in their own right. You also stood up for yourself without attacking the other person. If instead you responded aggressively by insulting their taste in music, the conversation may have escalated into an argument. Mutual validation allows you to assert yourself without making hurtful comments.

It's important to note that validating doesn't necessarily mean agreeing. You don't need to agree with your friend for ridiculing your music taste, because validation isn't a factual matter. It simply means understanding why someone might have an opposing viewpoint and recognizing that the viewpoint is legitimate (even if you don't see it the same way). In the example above, you don't need to agree with your friend's preference in order to see it as valid; you just need to understand that they're allowed to have an opinion different from yours and that's okay. Similarly, using mutual validation with your inner critic doesn't mean you have to agree that you're a loser or a failure. Sometimes, validating your inner critic is just about understanding its perspective or finding even a kernel of truth in what it's telling you.

Now that you know what mutual validation is, you can start using it with your inner critic. Remember, arguing with your inner critic isn't effective, even if it makes the most sense on the surface. Mutual validation will help you resist the urge to fight your inner critic by encouraging you to find a kernel of truth in your self-criticism (even if it's unkind) before you respond. It all starts with understanding what your inner critic is *trying* to say.

Validating Your Inner Critic

Validating your inner critic is a crucial first step in the process of making it more compassionate. Often, your self-criticism has some basis in truth but is overshadowed by cruelty, and it's your job to see past the harsh tone and understand what it's really trying to bring to your attention. To do that, it's helpful to imagine how the situation might be different if you had no self-criticism at all. Remember earlier in the chapter when we did this exercise around impulse shopping? It revealed that your inner critic caused you to question your actions and had a helpful outcome. At its root, this was its purpose even though the way it conveyed the criticism was exaggerated and disrespectful. Your inner critic might tell you that you're irresponsible and have no impulse control, for example, but if you're able to see through the shame and insults, you reveal accountability and values. While these insults probably aren't completely true, your inner critic said them for a reason. You can validate that you haven't been making the best choices, but you don't have to validate the harsh words.

Your validating response might be "I know I could be more disciplined with my spending. Since I feel bad about it, maybe I can put together a budget." Validating your inner critic is undoubtedly the counterintuitive approach. It seems like building your self-esteem should always involve disagreeing with your harsh inner critic. While an adversarial response—for example, "I'm allowed to buy whatever I want and I shouldn't feel bad about it"—may be true, it invalidates your own ability to evaluate yourself and identify mistakes or faults that you could improve on. It might also prompt your inner critic to push back with even more aggression in response. It's simply not as effective or as healthy to go the adversarial route. Self-compassion doesn't mean letting yourself off the hook every time you do something bad. Often, it involves having the self-discipline to keep yourself in check when you've stepped out of line. True self-compassion isn't always warm and fuzzy.

Instead, by validating the legitimate self-criticism hiding beneath the shame and hostility, you remove the harsh words. As long as your self-criticism has some truth to it, validation makes it more compassionate. That doesn't mean it will feel good; criticism never does. But that also doesn't mean it's bad.

When Your Inner Critic Gets It Completely Wrong

Most of the time, your self-criticism has some level of truth to it. It's usually just trying to give feedback to support your growth and self-discipline. And whenever there's even a kernel of truth to your self-criticism, you owe it to yourself to explore that truth, no matter how painful it may be. But sometimes your inner critic is so off-base that there doesn't seem to be any truth in what it's saying. This can be especially common in people who have experienced trauma or abuse. Usually, these self-criticisms are global evaluations and sometimes absurd-sounding, like "I'm useless trash" or "I have nothing to offer." Off-base thoughts like these are usually just a reaction to a painful or overwhelming emotion—they're not genuine criticisms. In cases like these, when you know your self-criticism is completely false, you should still avoid arguing with your inner critic. It's still possible to validate your inner critic, but that validation will look different. Here, you can validate the feeling behind the self-criticism rather than the message your inner critic is trying to convey. By saying to yourself, "This is coming from a place of fear/overwhelm/disappointment/frustration/ embarrassment," you can acknowledge your inner critic without arguing *or* agreeing with it.

Validating Yourself

You've recognized that your inner critic is valid for attempting to build your awareness of things you can improve on. But its insults and judgment are far from valid. And your rightfully hurt feelings in response are also valid. Acknowledge that too. So after you've validated your inner critic, you need to validate yourself. The good news is that you've already got some practice with this step under your belt because you learned how to validate yourself in chapter two. When your inner critic hurled nasty comments at you, you reminded yourself that you're worthy of respect.

Here's an example of what mutual validation may sound like using the impulse shopping example: "I know I haven't been spending more money than I want, and I recognize that. Since I feel bad about it, maybe I can make a budget and be more careful with my spending. BUT beating myself up over it doesn't undo the purchases I've already made. I deserve respect." By validating yourself, you're holding your inner critic accountable. Even though it's trying to help, it's doing it at the expense of your dignity. Although there are benefits to self-criticism, those benefits have limits.

Interestingly, people with low self-esteem often have more difficulty validating themselves than they do validating their inner critic. They often completely agree with their inner critic, so finding the validity in their self-criticism isn't a far leap. Validating themselves, on the other hand, is unnatural, especially when their inner critic seems to be "right."

Self-validation may seem difficult at first, but it doesn't have to be. In fact, you don't even have to tailor your self-validating statement to each individual situation. It can be the same scripted response each time. All that matters is that you believe whatever self-validation statement you use. Here are some examples:

> "But I don't deserve to speak to myself with such disrespect."
>
> "But shame isn't helping me improve."
>
> "But I'm doing the best I can."
>
> "But everybody makes mistakes, and I'll try harder next time."
>
> "But I can't expect myself to be perfect."
>
> "But that was a really hurtful way to make a point."
>
> "But beating myself up doesn't change what happened."

No matter what statement you use to validate yourself, don't forget the "but"! When using mutual validation in interpersonal contexts, it's generally best to avoid using the word "but" since it can be really invalidating and defeat the purpose. For example, "You did a great job, *but* I think you need to work on some things to improve it." The word "but" seems to negate the validation that came before it. However, when you use mutual validation in response to your inner critic, the word "but" helps you recognize that your worth takes precedence over any criticism your inner critic might hurl at you, no matter how valid it is.

There are countless ways to validate yourself, and they can either be specific to the situation or general and applicable to any situation. You can use any form of self-validation that's most helpful to you. If you find validating yourself difficult, choose one or two go-to validating statements that are easy for you to believe so that you don't need to think too hard about them. Sometimes it's hard to know which way is up while you're busy criticizing yourself, so having self-validation statements prepared in advance can be a huge help as you develop this new skill.

To really solidify the main points in this message, here are some more examples of mutual validation in response to self-criticism:

Self-critical thought: *I'm a slob because my house is a mess.*

What if my inner critic didn't exist: *I may never clean my house because I wouldn't care if it were messy.*

What my inner critic is trying to tell me: *I feel badly that my house isn't more presentable because I care about tidiness and organization.*

Validation of my inner critic: *Yes, inner critic, you're right that my house is a mess and I should probably clean it.*

Self-validation: *BUT I have been busy and stressed out and trying to balance other things. I want a clean home, but it's not in the cards for me right now.*

Self-critical thought: *I'm a failure because I failed my exam.*

What if my inner critic didn't exist: *I'd probably fail at everything since failure wouldn't bother me.*

What my inner critic is trying to tell me: *Failure bothers me because I want to do well when I put in effort.*

Validation of my inner critic: *I failed the exam, and now I know that next time I should study more or ask for help.*

Self-validation: *BUT just because I failed doesn't mean I'm a failure. Calling myself names doesn't change anything.*

Self-critical thought: *I'm a lazy bum because I don't work hard enough.*

What if my inner critic didn't exist: *I wouldn't care about hard work and probably would actually become quite lazy.*

What my inner critic is trying to tell me: *I feel bad about my low productivity because I value hard work.*

Validation of my inner critic: *It's true that I could do more, and it would be really nice if I put just a few more hours of work in.*

Self-validation: *BUT I am doing the best I can while trying to incorporate balance into my life so I can be effective at work.*

Here's an example of self-criticism that's completely false:

> **Self-critical thought**: *I'm a loser because I got rejected on a date. (Let's assume you can't think of anything you did wrong during the date.)*
>
> **Validation of my inner critic**: *This is coming from a place of disappointment.*
>
> **Self-validation**: *BUT I don't need to insult myself just because I'm disappointed.*

Self-Compassion Exercise:
Responding to Self-Criticism with Validation

Now it's your turn. When you have a self-critical thought, try using the mutual validation prompts on the next page in response to your self-criticism. I encourage you to write your responses to the prompts as you're getting started. Then, once you've got some practice, you can reflect internally, without any writing. You don't have to use this technique at the very moment when a self-critical thought arises. Using retrospect is completely acceptable. However, when you're able, it's beneficial to work through the steps when they feel immediately relevant. Give yourself some time to practice this exercise as needed and make sure you feel comfortable with the process before moving on to the next chapter. There you'll learn yet another approach for responding to a different form of self-criticism.

To download a free copy of this worksheet, visit rethinkyourself.info/worksheets or scan the QR code in the back of the book.

Self-critical thought:

_____

What my inner critic is trying to tell me:

_____

If my inner critic got it wrong, what painful emotion was it responding to?

_____

Validation of my inner critic:

_____

Self-validation:

_____

Self-critical thought:

_____

What my inner critic is trying to tell me:

_____

If my inner critic got it wrong, what painful emotion was it responding to?

_____

Validation of my inner critic:

_____

Self-validation:

_____

Chapter 9

Your Biggest Mistake Is Not Tolerating Them

A book about self-esteem would be criminally incomplete without a chapter on mistakes. That's because mistakes are often a huge source of self-criticism. Mistakes are supposed to be learning opportunities, but they feel more like personal indictments when you have low self-esteem. Your harsh inner critic magnifies your mistakes and minimizes your accomplishments, which, as we've seen, warps your self-concept into a fun-house mirror. Learning how to bounce back from your mistakes is a crucial step in flattening your fun-house mirror.

For the purpose of this chapter, a mistake is any action or inaction that results in an unintentional negative consequence. It's only clear that it was a mistake in hindsight, because if it were clear that you're making a mistake while you're making it, then it's not really a mistake. Sometimes mistakes occur due to factors that are outside of your control. For example, suppose you're baking a cake when you're interrupted by a phone call. Upon returning to your task, you forget to add eggs to the batter and as a result, the cake comes out of the oven flat, dense, and crumbly. Something clearly went wrong, and you didn't realize it until it was too late. But the mistake probably wouldn't have happened without the interruption. That part wasn't your fault.

If you have trouble tolerating your mistakes, then your initial reaction after realizing something went wrong with the cake might be to blame and insult yourself. You might call yourself a failure and tell yourself you can't do anything right. You might even conclude that you shouldn't bake again. The minor inconvenience of having a subpar cake would have turned into "evidence" of your incompetence. But this reaction, while bad for your self-esteem, also prevents you from investigating what went wrong and trying to learn from it. If this kind of reaction is a pattern, it begins to distort your perception of what mistakes are and what they say about you. Mistakes start to feel more impactful than they really are, and as a result you start to fear your mistakes rather than see them as a natural part of the learning process. Out of fear, you might pour your efforts into shielding yourself from the possibility of making a mistake. You may actively avoid situations that could lead to errors because the chance of failing is just too scary to stomach.

Paradoxically, by avoiding mistakes, we inadvertently give them more power. The more you avoid the possibility of failure, the more threatening failure feels. Your avoidance has conditioned you to believe you can't possibly tolerate your mistakes. After all, if you could tolerate them, why would you put so much effort into avoiding them?

The good news is that you don't have to avoid making mistakes in order to have self-esteem. Self-esteem isn't about finding the assurance that you'll never make a mistake again. After all, believing that you won't make a mistake is delusion, not confidence. Instead, confidence is about not letting mistakes hold power over you; it's about knowing how to tolerate them. But tolerating mistakes doesn't mean favoring them. Mistakes are always painful because they always have a negative consequence. Some are more painful than others, but none of them are ever fun. Nevertheless, learning how to tolerate mistakes and their consequences by resisting the urge to blame and insult yourself in response is an important step in building your self-esteem.

This chapter will teach you how to rethink your mistakes so that you can build some tolerance to them by letting go of unnecessary self-blame. You'll learn a technique to help you rethink any exaggerated or unfair self-talk in response to your mistakes. Rather than lying to yourself by downplaying your mistakes or playing into an impossible perfectionistic standard by trying to avoid them entirely, you'll learn how to be kind to yourself when you mess up. This will prevent your mistakes from warping your fun-house mirror.

The Three "Cons" of Mistakes

In this chapter, you'll learn to critically evaluate your internal reaction to mistakes in three key domains. I refer to them as the Three Cons, aptly named because each domain begins with the prefix "con": **con**sequence, **con**text, and **con**clusion. Their order is important, as each successive Con incorporates more depth and abstraction than the last. Each Con offers a different take on letting go of unnecessary self-blame, so it isn't always necessary that you use all three on any given occasion. If the first Con, the most concrete, is enough to convince you to let go of unnecessary self-blame, then you won't need to proceed to the next two. Some mistakes will call for a deeper level of analysis, which is what the second and third Cons are for. The third Con, the deepest and most abstract, is the most definitive as it doesn't allow for any self-blame, as long as the mistake was truly unintentional.

It might feel tempting to skip the first two Cons and rely solely on the third since the first two aren't always sufficient to reduce unnecessary self-blame in every circumstance. I advise against doing that because all three are important. They're meant to work together to help you build tolerance to your mistakes. Tolerance is about taking all necessary components of the mistake into account, not just the deepest and most existential. Not to mention, the more angles you use to analyze your mistakes, the more comprehensive and secure your tolerance to them will be.

The First Con: <u>Consequence</u>

The first Con invites you to critically and honestly examine the tangible consequence(s) of the mistake you made. Truly, many of our day-to-day mistakes have very minor or temporary consequences. If you spill a glass of water, the consequence is that you have to spend a few minutes cleaning up; if you make a wrong turn while driving, the consequence is that you reroute and your commute becomes ever-so-slightly longer; if you forget to grab an item while you're at the grocery store, the consequence is that you either go back or wait until the next time you head to the store to pick up the item. You get the point. There are countless mistakes that in the grand scheme of things are pretty minor. Earth-shattering, life-altering mistakes are incredibly rare. If you're particularly intolerant of your own mistakes, you might be afraid that you could make a catastrophic error at any moment, but that just isn't a realistic fear.

Despite most mistakes having relatively minor consequences, your harsh inner critic might exaggerate them. It's easy to think that after spilling a glass of water the rest of your day will be ruined, but this knee-jerk assumption is usually untrue. When you take a step back and ask yourself whether this is really that big of a deal, you realize you've made a mountain out of a molehill. And if you're used to criticizing yourself incessantly, you probably exaggerate the consequences of your mistakes purely out of habit. Analyzing the first Con of mistakes and being honest with yourself can help you break down that habit over time and slowly build your tolerance for making mistakes. Sometimes the consequences of a particular mistake are pretty substantial, and this step isn't asking you to overlook them if that's the case. But most day-to-day mistakes, while uncomfortable, aren't very consequential. When the consequence of a mistake is minor, what's the point of self-blame?

Mistakes can feel so damning because they tend to be glaring (at least to the person who made them). This makes them seem more meaningful and, therefore, harder to except. Did you notice the error in the previous sentence? If so, did you still understand the sentence? I put this error into the book intentionally to make a few important points about mistakes. The first point is that mistakes stand out, which makes them seem more common than they actually are. I doubt you've been impressed by my ability to spell and punctuate correctly through this book, and that's because spelling and punctuation are simply expected. But when an author messes up, it really stands out.

The second point is that mistakes don't always have dire consequences. Despite my "error," the sentence still delivered the intended message. It may not have been perfect, but it did its job. Most of the time, your mistakes will be the same. Imperfect but not catastrophic. On the other hand, maybe you didn't even notice the mistake until I pointed it out. If so, this is evidence that mistakes aren't always as obvious to others as they are to the person who made them. While the mistake appears glaring to me, maybe that's not the case for you, the reader. And maybe the same is true of some of your mistakes.

To practice using the first Con, all you really need to do is engage in critical thinking and a quick internal reflection. Truly, fifteen seconds of thought is completely sufficient, but feel free to dedicate more time to reflect if you prefer. Here are some questions you can ask yourself to facilitate the reflection process:

> Is my reaction to the mistake in proportion with its consequences?
>
> Will I remember this mistake tomorrow? Next week? Next month? Next year?
>
> Does this mistake have a clear impact on my or someone else's day or life?
>
> Is this mistake reparable? Are the consequences permanent?

The goal in analyzing the consequences of a mistake is not to explain away your mistake or ignore it. The goal is to ensure you aren't unfairly inflating the meaning or importance of your mistake. Treating every mistake, even the most minor, as a dire one can fan the flames of self-blame and lead you to feel like you can't do anything right. If you can recognize (when appropriate) that a mistake wasn't all that big, then you'll avert a whole lot of unnecessary self-blame.

Sometimes just this first Con is enough to help you keep your cool after making a mistake. For mistakes with minor or temporary consequences, the first Con reminds you that the mistake is tolerable and there's no good reason to be so harsh to yourself. If the first Con stopped your shame and blame spiral, there's really no need to move on to the second and third Cons unless you want to. You can end your analysis here. But some mistakes actually do have large and impactful consequences, which means they will trigger an appropriately large reaction. In those cases, the first Con won't offer much help in building your tolerance to your mistake or letting go of self-blame. Remember, the purpose of the first Con is to ensure that the size of your reaction is roughly equal to the size of the mistake. Whenever you need to deal with a big mistake, proceed to the second Con for a deeper and more abstract analysis.

The Second Con: <u>Context</u>

The second Con asks you to analyze the context of the mistake. By distributing the blame across all relevant factors, you can free yourself from some or all self-blame. There are plenty of times when context is a big part of why the mistake happened. For example, inaccurate or incomplete information might cause you to act or speak in a way that you wouldn't have with accurate and complete information; heightened emotions such as anger, fear, or anxiety might cloud your logical thinking or judgment, leading you to act recklessly or irrationally; seemingly unmanageable responsibilities or a burdensome workload might overwhelm normal thought processes, causing you to overlook or forget things. These contextual factors matter, as they can explain why a mistake happened and, as a result, take some of the blame off you.

No matter what your mistake was, one contextual factor that's always relevant is intent. Mistakes, by definition, are unintentional. So no matter the consequences of your mistake, you should always remind yourself that it wasn't on purpose. You had no ill intent. And that should certainly factor into whether or how much you blame yourself.

While considering the context of a mistake might divert some blame away from you and onto circumstantial factors, it's not intended to minimize or justify the mistake or shield you from its consequences; it's simply meant to help you more accurately and fairly explain the mistake, which places blame only where it's due. Every mistake has consequences, and those shouldn't be ignored. But just because you're the one who made the mistake doesn't mean you're completely at fault. Sometimes external factors lead to unfortunate outcomes, even if on the surface you seem to be responsible. However, in situations where you can't take full blame for the mistake, you're not necessarily off the hook. You can still assume responsibility for rectifying the consequences, just without the harsh self-criticism.

Like with the first Con, practicing the second Con really only requires some critical thinking and a quick internal reflection. Here are some reflection questions you can ask yourself:

> Is this a mistake I make often, or was this a one-time occurrence?
>
> Is there an external factor that might help explain why this mistake happened?
>
> If I could have changed one or two things about the situation, would I still have made the mistake?
>
> Is there anything that makes this mistake "forgivable"?

There are no right or wrong answers to these questions; they're meant to prompt critical thinking. Hopefully by considering the context around your mistake, you can minimize or even eliminate unnecessary self-blame. This builds your tolerance to your mistakes by preventing you from taking responsibility that isn't yours. Taking undue blame for a mistake can cause you to internalize a sense of failure or incompetence, which is clearly detrimental to your self-esteem.

While it's important to analyze contextual factors, it's not always enough. There may be some mistakes that just don't seem to have any contextual factors that minimize or remove self-blame. Sometimes you simply are the only one at fault and you have to accept that. Or maybe considering the context of your mistake does change your perception a bit, but not enough to tame your harsh inner critic. In that case, you can proceed to the third Con, which, as I stated previously, doesn't allow for any self-blame, as long as the mistake was truly unintentional.

The Third Con: <u>Conclusion</u>

The final Con involves taking a close look at the conclusion you made about your mistake. Almost always, this conclusion will be about you: you're a failure, you can't do anything right, you're unreliable, you're clumsy, and so on. You can draw on what you learned about shame in chapter 7, because the conclusions you make about your mistakes probably have a lot in common with shame: identification with the mistake, name-calling, and perception of permanence. If you notice any of these things in your conclusion, you'll have to rework your thoughts a bit.

If you've made it to the third Con, you've probably accepted that you made a mistake with a sizable consequence, absent any contextual factors that might alleviate blame, but you cannot and should not accept that you're bad or unworthy or any other negative conclusion because of it. If you're tempted to conclude that something is wrong with you (shame), you must challenge that conclusion.

Keep in mind that mistakes, by definition, imply that what happened was unintentional. That means there can never be malice in mistakes. Remembering this will help you limit the conclusion you reach after the mistake. You can't conclude that you're a bad person, for example, because you had no ill intentions. Some mistakes include other negative factors like bias or apathy, and while you should be aware of those factors, they also don't make you a bad person. That's not an appropriate conclusion to any singular mistake.

In chapter 7, you learned how to direct your attention to what you did wrong instead of what's wrong with you. Instead of calling yourself stupid for making a mistake, for example, you can conclude that the mistake you made was stupid, not that *you* are stupid.

When you try to only focus on a singular mistake, your harsh inner critic likes to play a trick on you by zooming way out and adding this mistake to a long list of others in order to make you look flawed or deficient. Even if that conclusion seems true, it's not relevant to the mistake in question. If you notice your harsh inner critic zooming out, it's important that you make an effort to zoom back in. It's okay to have weaknesses, but if you allow singular mistakes to be conflated with weaknesses, you'll have a hard time ever tolerating your mistakes since they'll always feel so much bigger than they actually are. If you continue to have trouble with conflating your mistakes with your character, take note of any relevant weaknesses so that you can examine them later, in chapter 11, where we'll focus on conceptualizing and accepting your limitations.

To put the third Con into practice, it's important to first determine what you're feeling compelled to conclude about yourself because of your mistake. Once you've done that, it's time to challenge your conclusion for being unreasonable, unfair, or both. Ask yourself the following questions:

> Did this one action single-handedly take away all of my good qualities?
>
> Was the single action so bad that it overshadowed all of my goodness?

The obvious answer to both these questions is no. When you recognize that your conclusion was unfair, give yourself permission to reject it. Remember, mistakes don't make you bad, they make you human. Give yourself the grace to be imperfect.

Similar to the second Con, the purpose here is not to let you off the hook. All mistakes have consequences, and you are accountable to those consequences. The goal of the third Con is to alleviate the burden of shame so that you can endure the consequences without undue suffering. Though the mistake may still result in pain, the pain is more tolerable when you take the shame away.

Putting It All Together

Simply knowing the Three Cons doesn't necessarily mean you can apply them to yourself. When you're so used to blaming yourself after making any mistake, it can be pretty difficult to retrain your brain. It's common to feel defensive of your inner critic, wanting to agree with it, and even believing that you deserve to beat yourself up. Oddly enough, you might have a much easier time extending grace to others when they make a mistake than you do to yourself. Something about giving yourself compassion can feel really daunting. If that's how you feel, you can start by getting some practice with the Three Cons by applying them to other people's mistakes before you even address your own. That way, you can get acquainted with the process and practice critical analysis without the intimidation of taking on your own self-criticism.

Maybe start looking out for mistakes that people around you make, and practice applying the Three Cons to those. Once you've developed some mental muscle memory, you can start to apply them to your own mistakes. At that point, you'll feel more confident in your ability to use this technique, which will help you feel more comfortable tolerating the discomfort of challenging your self-critical thoughts.

Practicing applying this approach to the mistakes of others doesn't have to involve people you know, or even real people for that matter! Mistakes are often a central element to the plot of television shows, movies, and books. If you look for them, examples of mistakes aren't hard to find.

To really illustrate how to apply the Three Cons, I'll walk you through a detailed example of a familiar mistake depicted in television and film: a kid playing baseball in the backyard accidentally shatters the kitchen window with the baseball. After the glass shatters, panic sets in and self-criticism seems inevitable. The Three Cons provide a different perspective, making it easier to extend compassion and let go of blame. Let's apply them to this scenario.

The First Con: Consequence

The obvious consequence of this mistake is a broken window. Depending on the financial situation of the family, that consequence could be substantial or minor. The consequence might be exacerbated if the ball also caused damage to the interior of the house by putting a hole in a wall or breaking a piece of furniture. Even worse, if the ball struck someone inside the house, they may have sustained an injury. The most direct consequence for the kid is probably some sort of punishment like getting grounded or being expected to take on extra chores to pay for the damage. Of course, the exact consequences would depend on the specific circumstances of the mistake.

While the consequences of the mistake certainly aren't insignificant, the visceral reaction to hearing the glass shatter can lead to some serious catastrophizing. Most likely, the consequences won't last very long and may eventually be forgotten. The window and any broken furniture will be replaced, and the kid will eventually regain their freedom after being grounded. Looking at the first Con can reduce a lot of unnecessary self-blame. In this example, the first Con is certainly helpful, but it doesn't quite feel like enough, so let's proceed to the second Con to explore the mistake in more depth and abstraction.

The Second Con: Context

There could be a number of contextual factors at play in this mistake. Maybe the kid had played baseball in the backyard numerous times without incident. Maybe they even had permission from their parent to play baseball because the risk of damage seemed low. Maybe they were trying to be responsible by aiming away from the house, but they just happened to hit a fly ball that went directly for the window.

Regardless of other contextual factors, in almost any example involving this mistake, we can be sure that the kid meant no harm. Of course, this doesn't relieve the kid of the consequences of their mistake. They still need to take responsibility for their unintentional actions and take the necessary steps to rectify the harm they caused. Since they intended a different outcome and even took precautions to prevent the mistake from happening, harsh self-criticism doesn't feel particularly appropriate. Looking at the context of the situation chips away at the immediate perception of absolute blame. But if you're not fully convinced by this perspective on the situation, you can proceed to the third Con for further analysis.

The Third Con: Conclusion

A potential conclusion to the broken window example could be that the kid is a burden, a failure, can't do anything right, and maybe even should give up on baseball entirely. But the third Con asks us to consider whether these conclusions are fair and reasonable. We all may hold slightly different opinions on this determination, but I believe that no matter how seemingly disastrous the mistake might seem, it doesn't automatically, by itself, make the kid bad. Or exempt the kid from forgiveness. And if you agree with me on this one, you can't fairly or reasonably draw conclusions about the kid's character, value, or worth *based on this singular mistake*. To reiterate an earlier point in the chapter, this doesn't justify or explain away the mistake; the mistake still happened and had consequences. It simply takes away our license to inflate the mistake into unfair judgments about the person who made the mistake, which is exactly the point of this exercise.

Conspicuous Mistakes

The Three Cons exercise is straightforward for mistakes nobody is around to witness. But mistakes don't always happen in vacuums. The possibility of ridicule and judgment from others is often what makes mistakes seem so threatening. Since this book is about self-esteem, self-judgment is really all that *should* matter, but we can't deny that interpersonal criticism often plays a big role too. Whenever your mistakes are visible to others and you notice a fear of judgment arising within you, take note of the following points and repeat them to yourself.

- **You shouldn't base your self-concept on other people's perceptions of you.** This is of course easier said than done. You must tolerate that other people sometimes don't extend you the compassion and forgiveness that you're trying to extend to yourself, but that shouldn't delegitimize your own efforts. Remember that when you allow the criticism of others to influence your self-esteem, you'll begin to require external validation to build and maintain your self-esteem. That's a dangerous thing to do.
- **You can be open to feedback from others, but you get to decide what to do with that feedback.** You don't need to take criticism that's meant to tear you down. If you receive constructive criticism, you can use it to learn and grow. If the criticism is mean-spirited, harsh, or untrue, it's okay to reject it.
- **It's okay to be embarrassed.** Even if nobody else is outwardly ridiculing you, you might fear that they're judging you internally. Recognize that everyone has made mistakes and therefore everyone knows how it feels to be embarrassed by them. You can tolerate embarrassment. It's not a sign that you're flawed, it's just an uncomfortable feeling.

Self-Compassion Exercise:
Building Tolerance to Your Mistakes

Now you try. Identify mistakes you've made recently and write them in the spaces on the next page. Then, using the Three Cons, analyze each mistake to recalibrate your reaction to them. The mistakes you use as examples don't need to be huge. Any mistakes your harsh inner critic latches onto are fine. After all, sometimes your harsh inner critic blows minor mistakes out of proportion.

If you find this to be too difficult right now, practice on other people's mistakes first. Watch a movie or television show or read a novel and write down mistakes the characters make, then analyze those. But don't move on to the next chapter until you're able to use the Three Cons on your own mistakes with relative ease and comfort. Take all the time you need; there's no rush.

Your analysis doesn't have to immediately follow your mistakes. Hours or even days later is perfectly fine. Sometimes you just don't have the time or mental capacity to do all this while you're still dealing with the consequences of the mistake. That's okay.

To download a free copy of this worksheet, visit rethinkyourself.info/worksheets or scan the QR code in the back of the book.

Mistake: _____

Consequence of the mistake:

_____

Does the severity of your self-criticism match the severity of the mistake and its consequences? (yes or no) _____

Context of the mistake:

_____

Does the context of the mistake remove all or some self-blame? (yes or no) _____

Conclusion(s) you made about the mistake:

_____

Is the conclusion fair and reasonable? (yes or no) _____

Mistake: _____

Consequence of the mistake:

_____

Does the severity of your self-criticism match the severity of the mistake and its consequences? (yes or no) _____

Context of the mistake:

_____

Does the context of the mistake remove all or some self-blame? (yes or no) _____

Conclusion(s) you made about the mistake:

_____

Is the conclusion fair and reasonable? (yes or no) _____

Chapter 10

The Benefit of the Doubt

Is she mad at me? Is this my fault? Did I offend him?

When you're not really sure if you did something wrong, your head begins to buzz with questions. As you try to answer them, your thoughts get taken over by self-criticisms for all the things you might have done wrong. But you can't respond to this type of self-criticism using the techniques you've learned so far, because all you really have to work with are assumptions.

This chapter focuses on the final technique to help you rethink your self-criticism: giving the benefit of the doubt. You've learned several techniques to respond to your inner critic with compassion after you've done something that doesn't measure up to your standards. Up to now, the focus has been on situations when it's clear (or at least reasonably clear) that you were in the wrong. But things don't always work out in such a straightforward way. It isn't always obvious whether you've actually done anything wrong or not.

Life is full of ambiguity, and most of us don't like that very much. We crave certainty, and some of us will go to great lengths to avoid the discomfort of not knowing. It's why we explore, ask questions, form hypotheses, and seek answers. But no matter how much we hate uncertainty, it's simply a part of life and we can't avoid it completely.

It's not always obvious on the surface, but people with low self-esteem often resort to self-blame in the face of uncertainty. For example, imagine you just received a passive-aggressive email from your boss. You aren't sure why they're using this tone and aren't aware of anything you've done wrong. It's kind of unsettling to think that your boss is upset and you don't know why. Despite having no evidence to accept blame, you might assume your boss is mad at you for something, that their passive-aggressive tone is your fault. This assumption gives your inner critic permission to judge and criticize anything it wants, since you can't point to any specific thing you did wrong. Maybe it's because you don't work hard enough. Maybe you made a mistake on your last report. Maybe you ask stupid questions. Maybe you forgot to complete some important task. Maybe you're annoying . . . Before you know it, you're deep in a shame spiral, fixating on flaws and mistakes that may not even exist. You've completely ignored the possibility that your boss might just be having a bad day, or they're just a bad communicator. Although there are plenty of possibilities that have nothing to do with you, the uncertainty gave way to unnecessary self-blame.

The Threat of Uncertainty and the Safety of Self-Blame

Maybe the above example of the passive-aggressive email feels all too familiar. Or maybe you've never noticed that you tend to blame yourself before you can be certain you were truly at fault. It's actually a pretty common reaction to uncertainty, especially for people with low self-esteem. When things are unclear, it's tempting to jump to the conclusion that you must be to blame for something. That's because blaming yourself sometimes brings less discomfort than having no conclusion to jump to at all.

At face value, the temptation to blame yourself without evidence doesn't seem to make any sense. Why would something so self-destructive be such an instinctual reaction to ambiguity? Despite how maladaptive it seems, self-criticism in this context can actually serve as a self-protective measure (albeit not a very healthy or effective one). That's because uncertainty is often so unbearable that self-blame feels like a better alternative.

Uncertainty is an inherently vulnerable state because it leaves us powerless. It provokes a sense of anxiety by telling us we need to tread carefully because danger could arise unexpectedly from anywhere at any time. How can we control the outcome of a situation if we don't even have the information we need to assess it accurately? It's a very uncomfortable feeling, and most people try very hard to avoid it.

Since uncertainty is so distressing, many of us feel a strong urge to do whatever we can to gain certainty and, by extension, control. Self-blame is an easy way to take control over an uncertain situation because it convinces you that the circumstances are your own doing. By taking responsibility, you now have the power to do something about it (at least that's what you tell yourself).

If you decide that your boss sent the passive-aggressive email because you don't work hard enough, you can rectify the situation by being more productive. Even if this explanation is entirely wrong, it brought you a sense of control that defused the threat of uncertainty. Self-blame doesn't feel good, but at least it's familiar, and sometimes the devil you know is better than the devil you don't.

The problem, as you can probably see, is that the control you get from self-blame is just an illusion. If you were wrong about the reason for the passive-aggressive email, working harder won't change anything. The perception of control gave you a sense of peace, but it came at a cost.

Seeking control in an uncertain situation has a trade-off. Self-blame is certainly an effective way to reduce ambiguity in the short-term, and that benefit is valid, even if it's misguided. But unsurprisingly, self-blame sacrifices your self-esteem and, as a result, your overall well-being. That's the consequence of incessant unearned self-blame.

When it's spelled out this way, self-blame as a certainty-seeking method just doesn't seem to be worth its negative consequences. So why do people do it? It's likely because anxiety tends to be shortsighted. If there's an immediate threat (like uncertainty), we often only focus on limiting that immediate threat, even if our actions just lead to larger, longer-term threats. Humans don't always behave rationally, but there's usually a reason for their behavior. In this case, the reason for unnecessary self-blame is to avoid a short-term threat, even if it's not helpful in the long-term (because it comes at the expense of your self-esteem).

Other than alleviating anxiety, self-blame in the face of uncertainty can also serve to protect us against the possibility of criticism from others. Instead of waiting for your boss to tell you everything you did wrong, you can unload on yourself first. That way, if your boss does call you into their office, their criticism won't sting as badly since you beat them to the punch. You've emotionally prepared yourself for the worst-case scenario, and you won't be completely shattered by any criticism that comes out of left field (that's the hope, at least). Maybe this approach works *sometimes*, but what if your boss never actually criticizes you? Now you've criticized yourself for no reason, and your self-esteem has taken an unnecessary hit.

Not only is self-blame unhelpful at seeking certainty, but often, seeking certainty isn't even helpful in and of itself because it brings with it another trade-off between control and freedom. There are many, many aspects of our lives that are outside of our control, probably more than are within our control. To live functioning lives, we need to accept that fact. Attempting to take control over every aspect of your life would severely limit your agency.

For example, getting into a car comes at the risk of being involved in a car accident, so if you want to make sure you never get into a car accident, you could just never get into a car. But you could also be involved in a car accident as a pedestrian, so by that logic you should avoid sidewalks too. Meeting new people comes at the risk of being rejected or even experiencing the pain of loss after you've grown close, so to avoid ever facing rejection or loss, you could simply isolate yourself from anyone who could hurt you (i.e., everyone). When you take it to an extreme, it's easy to see how attempting to take complete control involves giving something else up—the freedom to do what you want with your life.

Of course, few of us take control to this extreme, so the amount of freedom we give up is smaller and less apparent. But it still exists. When you try to take control over uncertainty by blaming yourself, you forfeit your ability to assess the facts of the situation rationally.

When faced with uncertainty, the most adaptive thing you can do is accept what you don't know. Acceptance is admittedly very difficult since it requires you to overcome an instinctual urge to grasp for control. But acknowledging your urge to control shouldn't feel like an indictment. The word "control" usually carries a negative connotation, but the truth is we all need some element of control over our lives in order to maintain our well-being. Control isn't a bad thing; it's a basic emotional need. But knowing when to let go of control and accept uncertainty is a necessary step not only in developing emotional stability but also in building your self-esteem.

Accepting Uncertainty

As you can see, building your self-esteem requires you to be willing to accept a lack of control. Without this willingness, you'll always face the temptation to blame yourself to avoid the threat of uncertainty. But uncertainty, while uncomfortable, is often not as threatening as it seems. In this section you'll learn how to accept uncertainty by using three steps: 1) call it out, 2) identify other possibilities, and 3) make space for the uncertainty.

Keep in mind that acceptance can come in many forms. The focus of this chapter is only on the specific circumstances of uncertainty that cause the urge to blame yourself. Other types of acceptance, like accepting a chronic illness or the death of a loved one, are best addressed in other ways and covered in other self-help books and even many forms of therapy.

Step 1: Call It Out

The first step in accepting uncertainty is to identify and name what's happening as soon as you notice it. This is the simplest and most straightforward of the three steps, but surprisingly it can also be the most impactful. When you notice yourself feeling tempted to blame yourself unfairly, challenge your self-blame by saying the following statement to yourself:

"I'm blaming myself as a defense against uncertainty."

For example, imagine you're catching up with a friend over dinner, but your friend seems to be in a bad mood. You aren't sure why, and maybe you're even too timid to ask. You notice yourself analyzing what you've done so you can figure out whether your friend is mad at you. Your inner critic generates piles of evidence confirming that your friend's sour mood is because of you. Once you notice yourself making this assumption, say to yourself, "I'm blaming myself as a defense against uncertainty." By blaming yourself, you're taking responsibility for your friend's mood so you can tell yourself that you have the power to change it. But it might not be your responsibility anyway. As you now know, this grab for control isn't actually as helpful as it seems at first.

You can certainly inquire about your friend's mood if you really want to be sure. If it has nothing to do with you, it's nice to have that confirmed. It's also nice to check in with your friend simply because you care about them. But even with verbal confirmation, you might still wonder if your friend is afraid to be honest that you did dampen their mood. If that's the case, you're back at square one. Instead, try to trust that your friend will bring issues to your attention if they really need to. It's their responsibility to speak up for themselves, not your responsibility to read their mind.

It's interesting to think about this attempt at seizing control as an ironic form of narcissism. When you boil it all down, it stems from an assumption that everything is about you. When something goes wrong, it's your fault. When things seem off, you must be tainting the vibe. It's strange that self-criticism can inspire an inflated sense of self-importance. As odd as it may sound in a self-help book about self-esteem, this is one (possibly the only) situation when it might be helpful to remind yourself you're not *that* important. It's a humbling realization, but it might also remind you not to assume everything is your fault.

This step is all about resisting the urge to take responsibility for something that might not be yours. It's also about being honest with yourself and admitting that you don't actually know all the details of a situation. Making assumptions that you're to blame gets in the way of accepting the uncertainty, because it's an attempt to avoid ambiguity in favor of certainty.

Step 2: Identify Other Possibilities

After calling out your intention to seek certainty, the next step is to determine other possible explanations for the situation. Your assumption that you're at fault is only one possible explanation, but there could be others that have nothing to do with you. Since you don't know for sure, it's just as reasonable to give yourself the benefit of the doubt as it is to blame yourself.

The goal of this step is for you to balance your perspective. When you assume you're at fault, your perspective is skewed. Not only are you assuming the worst, you're also assuming the situation involves you. But you shouldn't overlook alternative explanations. You don't need to ignore the possibility that you're at fault; you just need to acknowledge that it's one of many possibilities, so you can't make a definitive conclusion.

To identify other possibilities, you have to externalize the blame. For example, imagine that after going on a first date, the other person blocks you and doesn't respond to any of your messages. It might be tempting to assume they ghosted you because you did something wrong. But your assumption fails to recognize external possibilities. Maybe your date realized they weren't ready for dating and were too timid to tell you the truth. Maybe they misunderstood something that happened on the date. Maybe they found someone else and didn't want to keep talking to other dates. Maybe they're just a bad communicator. There could even be positive explanations for what happened too, though you might find these harder to believe. Maybe they tend to go for people who are bad for them, and your positive qualities turned them off. Maybe something about you was intimidating and made them feel insecure. Whatever possibilities you can come up with, all that matters is that you acknowledge that you being at fault is nothing more than a hypothesis. That hypothesis *may* be true, but you shouldn't assume without concrete evidence.

The point of identifying other possibilities isn't to evaluate each one so you can determine which is the most likely explanation, or to do detective work to prove your assumptions right or wrong. It's not to replace a negative explanation with a positive one. It's to drive home the point that you don't know all the details of the situation for certain, which will help broaden your perspective so you stop having tunnel vision toward self-blame. There are countless other possibilities, so it's irrational to make assumptions about which one is true. You simply don't know. Not knowing is uncomfortable, and this step isn't meant to resolve the discomfort of uncertainty. That's okay, because the next step is meant to help you tolerate it.

It might be helpful for you to phrase all your possibilities using words like "maybe" or "what if."

> Maybe my boss is just having a bad day.
>
> What if my friend's mood has nothing to do with me?
>
> Maybe my date realized they're not ready for dating.

This reminds you that you're not trying to find certainty where it doesn't exist but simply accepting that you don't know the answer. Part of accepting is being honest with yourself about what you don't know.

Step 3: Make Space for the Uncertainty

In the final step, you'll let go of your desire to have an explanation and accept that it's okay not to know. The first two steps were meant to challenge your perception, but this one is meant to help you tolerate the uncertainty. With that said, acceptance usually doesn't happen right away; it definitely requires some practice and patience.

Acceptance can mean many different things, and most people have slightly different ideas about what acceptance is. To make sure you have a solid understanding, let's quash a few myths right from the beginning.

- **Acceptance does not mean you have to like something.** You're not required to like uncertainty, because that's not the point.
- **Acceptance does not mean accepting that you're wrong.** Since you're dealing with uncertainty, you can't accept that you're wrong because you don't know that.

Acceptance just means allowing for uncertainty and tolerating the discomfort that comes with it. It involves resisting the urge to construct a narrative that gives you the illusion of certainty, and instead choosing to acknowledge that you do not, and in some cases *cannot*, know the answer.

Acceptance is the opposite of avoidance. When there's no definitive evidence, self-blame is an attempt to avoid uncertainty, and accepting that you don't know is choosing to face it. In this way, acceptance is an active process and doesn't happen by chance. To work toward acceptance, you have to let go of your desire to control. You need to adopt the mindset that not having total control is tolerable and sometimes even healthy. That's much easier said than done, but using an acceptance statement can help.

Acceptance statements remind you to make room for uncertainty. Choose an acceptance statement to repeat to yourself whenever acceptance is necessary. Think of acceptance statements as the building blocks for more adaptive beliefs about uncertainty. If you repeat it enough times, the statement will eventually start to feel like an authentic expression of your core beliefs. Below is a list of acceptance statements, but feel free to create your own statement as well.

"Not knowing is uncomfortable, but I can tolerate it."

"Uncertainty will not kill me."

"I've dealt with uncertainty before, and I can deal with this."

"I'm capable of accepting uncertainty."

"It's okay to feel discomfort when I'm uncertain."

"I don't know what's happening, but I can accept the situation."

"I can be kind to myself in ambiguous situations."

Choose a statement that resonates most with you and designate it your new acceptance belief. Make sure it's one you can agree with on some level. Each time you're faced with uncertainty, use your acceptance statement to let go of your urge to self-deprecate as an attempt to take control. Take some slow, calming breaths and try to release any tension you feel in your body by relaxing your muscles. Try to be open to absorbing the meaning of your acceptance statement's words. Your harsh inner critic might try to subvert your efforts with a list of "what-ifs," but just keep reminding yourself of what you're working toward and eventually you'll have a little more strength to resist the urge to find an explanation.

Adopting new beliefs, or undertaking any type of change, requires intentional repetition, so it'll take some time. After all, there's a big gap between avoidance and acceptance. It's not a light switch; it's a process. You'll need to repeat your acceptance statement a lot for it to really stick. Just like excelling at playing the piano requires practicing the same songs over and over and running a marathon requires training for it, if you want to accept uncertainty, you'll have to be persistent.

Self-Compassion Exercise:
Accepting Uncertainty

Now that you're familiar with the steps of accepting uncertainty, it's time to put them into practice. From now on, be on the lookout for times when you blame yourself for things without conclusive evidence. When you notice it happening, practice the three steps of accepting uncertainty. Give yourself the benefit of the doubt. Be kind to yourself when there's no clear reason not to.

1. **Call it out**

   "I'm blaming myself as a shield against uncertainty."

2. **Identify other possibilities**

   Use words like *"maybe"* and *"what if."*

   "I'm not that important."

   "Not everything is about me."

3. **Make space for the uncertainty**

   Use your acceptance statement and repeat it as many times as you need.

   Take slow, calming breaths and try to release any tension you feel in your body.

   Be patient. You may not be very good at this step right away.

Chapter 11

———

The Bad and the Ugly

You have imperfections. Everyone does. And it often feels like they're what stand between you and a strong self-esteem. Wouldn't self-compassion be so much easier if you were perfect? The truth is, you'll always have traits you don't like, and if you want to build your self-esteem, you've got to grapple with that reality. While it's important to know your strengths to build your self-esteem, it's also important to hold space for your weaknesses.

This might seem like a strange topic in a book about self-esteem. After all, the purpose of this book is to help you feel better about yourself, and focusing on your weaknesses doesn't seem to accomplish that goal. But your weaknesses are an important part of your self-concept, and you shouldn't ignore them. People with low self-esteem often misrepresent or exaggerate their weaknesses, which, as we've seen, warps their self-concept like a fun-house mirror. The solution isn't to fabricate an illusion of perfection. Instead, it's to develop an accurate sense of self and not allow your weaknesses to overshadow your strengths. It's important to see your weaknesses for what they are, and learn how to not feel threatened by them. Once you get a clear picture of who you really are, maybe you'll have more appreciation for what you see— imperfections and all.

It can be hard to understand why addressing your weaknesses is necessary for building self-esteem. Most of us would probably rather ignore them. While this is the strategy many use to build their self-esteem, it's not a helpful one. To understand why, think about the amount of attention you give to your weaknesses as a spectrum between fixating on and ignoring them.

Fixating on your weaknesses		Ignoring your weaknesses
Low self-esteem	**Healthy self-esteem**	Low self-esteem

One end of the spectrum involves fixating on or obsessing over your weaknesses. This is what most of us imagine when we think about low self-esteem: people who tend to exaggerate their weaknesses and even feel consumed by them. They have difficulty acknowledging their positive qualities because all they see in themselves is deficiency. If you spend a lot of time on this end of the spectrum, maybe you were hoping this book would teach you how to stop thinking so much about your weaknesses. But as you'll see, that approach isn't as helpful as you might think.

The other end of the spectrum involves ignoring, minimizing, or downplaying your weaknesses. This end is just as strongly associated with low self-esteem as the other, but we don't often think of it that way. Truly, the only reason someone would feel the need to downplay or hide their weaknesses is because they feel threatened by them. If you find yourself on this end of the spectrum, maybe you fear that your weaknesses make you more susceptible to self-criticism, and the only way to be confident is to act like you're perfect. But everybody has weaknesses, and pretending you don't warps your mirror just as much as overmagnifying them does: it causes you to fear certain parts of yourself, making self-reflection practically unbearable. Ignoring what you don't like doesn't make it go away—in fact, it only gives it more power.

The ideal amount of attention you should give to your weaknesses is somewhere in the middle. Here, you acknowledge your weaknesses when it's relevant or beneficial to do so, but you don't fixate on them. You tolerate your weaknesses even if you wish you could change them. You think about them in a way that's accurate and fair. You acknowledge that you're imperfect, but it doesn't threaten your ego because you know you have plenty of positive qualities as well. You also know that having imperfections, in and of itself, doesn't make you inferior to others (because everyone has them!). Acknowledging your weaknesses is an important part of being a self-aware, balanced, and humble person.

This chapter will help you think about your weaknesses in a healthy and productive way. To start, you'll need to make a list of your negative traits. Take a few moments and write down some of your unhealthy, unfavorable, embarrassing, or just plain ugly personality traits. Don't include any appearance-based traits, though. We're just focusing on who you are, not what you look like. Try to limit yourself to only 10 weaknesses for now. You don't *have* to identify that many, but you certainly shouldn't go past ten. If you don't set a cap on this exercise, you'll risk spiraling around everything that's wrong with you. So be choosy about which weaknesses you identify; you could start with the ones that feel the most meaningful or representative of your character, or with the less substantial ones so you don't feel too overwhelmed. There's no right or wrong, just what feels best to you.

_____   _____

_____   _____

_____   _____

_____   _____

_____   _____

Rethinking Your Weaknesses

Now that you have a list of your weaknesses, you can start to rethink them by learning how to conceptualize them in a way that's fair, accurate, and, most importantly, kind. This chapter will teach you seven methods to accomplish that task. However, keep in mind that the point isn't to disprove your weaknesses, just to ensure they're accurate and fair. Doing that will prevent you from letting your weaknesses define you or overshadow your strengths. Then, you'll be more willing to acknowledge them in a healthy way without feeling threatened by them.

Not all of these methods will work for every weakness, so use your discretion to employ whatever method feels most fitting for any particular situation. You may even decide to combine a few methods to really make sure you're getting the most out of the chapter. Use your intuition, and use whatever approaches make sense. There's no right way to do it.

1. Be Specific

The best way to ensure you don't misrepresent your weaknesses is to be as specific as possible about exactly what they are. People with low self-esteem often exaggerate their weaknesses by making broad, sweeping statements about them. Describing your weaknesses this way makes them seem a lot more substantial than they really are, which warps your self-concept. Instead, make sure you think about your weaknesses fairly and accurately to flatten your fun-house mirror.

Let's use the word "annoying" as an example. What does being "annoying" actually entail? Does it mean exhibiting dependent tendencies? Asking too many questions? Having an overly pessimistic attitude? Whatever the case may be, accurately identifying what this trait entails will help you conceptualize it in clearer and less absolute terms. This also prevents you from inflating its severity, relevance, or impact. As a result, the trait becomes a lot less threatening to your self-esteem without needing to downplay it.

Another way to be specific about your weaknesses is to look for exceptions. It's highly unlikely that you exhibit each of your weaknesses in every context, so ask yourself in which contexts you *don't* struggle with a particular weakness. For example, if one of your weaknesses is that you struggle with assertiveness, think about times when assertiveness isn't an issue for you. Maybe you're more assertive at work and less assertive with friends and family or vice versa. Or maybe you're more assertive with people of equal status and find it harder to assert yourself to authority figures. Keeping in mind that many of your weaknesses are only relevant in specific contexts helps you narrow down their scope and make them feel less threatening. Just remember, the purpose in looking for exceptions isn't to disprove any of your weaknesses. After all, exceptions don't disprove anything. They do, however, help you see beyond the weakness. If you're used to thinking of yourself in overly negative terms, you probably tend to think of your weaknesses in absolute or universal terms, which usually misrepresents them.

2. No Name-Calling

It's pretty obvious why you should avoid calling yourself names. Besides being mean-spirited, it's also one of the markers of shame. It should be no surprise that calling yourself nasty names warps your fun-house mirror.

Name-calling implies a negative connotation that's intended to disparage. It stings. For example, the term *control freak* is a lot more mean-spirited than *particular* or *apprehensive*. And even though *particular* and *apprehensive* aren't exactly compliments, they don't quite have the sting that a more pejorative term like *control freak* has. Remember, the goal of this chapter is not to somehow repackage your weaknesses as strengths. It's simply to ensure that the way you conceptualize them is fair and kind.

Look through your list of weaknesses and determine whether any involve name-calling. Ask yourself whether you would use this wording if you were talking about someone you care about. If the answer is no, then you shouldn't say it about yourself either. You deserve just as much of your own compassion as your loved ones do. To come up with alternative wording for these weaknesses, think of similar ways to describe them, still in an accurate way but without such hurtful or loaded terms. You don't need to downplay your weaknesses; just make sure you're not insulting yourself. To help you out, here are a few examples:

Cheapskate → Frugal

Coward → Cautious/Timid/Hesitant

Careless slob → Inattentive/Forgetful

Lazy bum → Low energy/Low motivation

3. Understand How You Compensate for Your Weaknesses

Everyone has weaknesses, and yet somehow we all seem to manage in spite of them. That's because we sometimes find ways to adapt to our weaknesses so we can live our lives. For some weaknesses, you might have a counteracting strength that compensates for them, and you may not even realize it. For example, if you have a bad memory, you might compensate by keeping detailed notes or developing advanced planning skills so you don't have to rely on your poor memory. Here are a few more examples:

Bad at managing uncertainty → Good at planning

Bad at multitasking → Good with time management

Staying mindful of how you compensate for your weaknesses diminishes their power over you. They feel a lot less limiting when you have a counter-acting strength to help you overcome them. But if you don't consider how you compensate for your weaknesses, you might feel less capable than you really are. Just look at the difference between these two statements.

> "I struggle with uncertainty."
>
> "I struggle with uncertainty, but I make up for it with my planning skills."

The first example makes a definitive point about a weakness, while the second one emphasizes that the weakness isn't restrictive. Consider whether you've found ways to compensate for any of your weaknesses. How much do those weaknesses really hold you back? Even though you'd like to improve them, they probably don't render you completely incapable.

4. Avoid Universals

In chapter 5, you learned how all-or-nothing thinking can diminish your self-esteem. It's a mental trap many people find themselves in, and it's often the source of unfair standards that make you feel inadequate. The trick to over-coming all-or-nothing thinking is exploring the space between "all" and "noth-ing" and remembering that one or two exceptions don't necessarily disprove a fact.

To do this with your weaknesses, first recognize that most likely, your weak-nesses don't apply to all contexts. When you talk or think about your weak-nesses in universal terms, it's hard not to feel defeated. Look out for extreme words such as "always," "never," "everything," and "nothing." Those are strong indicators that you're thinking about your weaknesses in exaggerated and universal terms.

Instead, you can use qualitative indicators like "sometimes," "can be," or even "frequently." Adding these qualifiers to your weaknesses is a simple way to demonstrate that they're not a universal truth, just an observed pattern. It feels a whole lot less all-encompassing and intimidating that way. No matter what your weaknesses are, it's always (yes, always) unfair to make such de-finitive statements about them.

5. State It as an Opinion, Not a Fact

There's nothing wrong with viewing your weaknesses as facts; perhaps many or even all of them are. As I said before, the presence of weaknesses shouldn't threaten your self-esteem. But even though your weaknesses are [probably] factual, there are a few reasons you might want to view them as opinions.

First, stating your weaknesses as opinions rather than facts reminds you that your perception of yourself is subjective and may in fact be warped. And that reminder helps you be more open to the possibility that you could be wrong about some of your weaknesses. Have you ever considered that what you perceive as a weakness might not actually be a weakness? Maybe you're so hard on yourself, or your standards are so high, that some of your weaknesses are only evident to you. What if your self-concept is so distorted it's causing you to see things that aren't really there? If that's the case, then an important step in changing your perception of that weakness is acknowledging that your self-concept is, by definition, subjective. Others may see you differently, and as I said in chapter 6, you should be open to the perspectives of others if you want to change your self-concept.

Second, viewing your weaknesses as opinions is helpful because opinions are more flexible than facts. Facts don't change. If you think of yourself as disorganized, for example, then stating this as a fact gives it legitimacy and permanence. You're disorganized, and that's just how it is. On the other hand, viewing it as an opinion gives you permission to change your mind, if appropriate. Stating, "I think of myself as being disorganized" casts a little bit of doubt on your perception of yourself, allowing room for other possibilities.

Here are more examples of phrases you can use to think of your weaknesses as opinions rather than facts:

> "I'm not friendly" → "I don't see myself as friendly"
>
> "I'm uptight" → "I think of myself as uptight"
>
> "I'm cynical" → "I believe I'm cynical"

After consistently thinking about your weaknesses as subjective opinions, you might be surprised how your perception of them changes over time. After all, changing your perception of yourself is the goal. Why not give it a shot?

6. Use the Job Interview Technique

"What are your weaknesses?" This classic job interview question most people are advised to prepare for can be a minefield. Of course, you want to convince the interviewer to hire you by making yourself look good, even when discussing your weaknesses, but the cliché answer "My greatest weakness is that I care too much" usually doesn't go over well with employers. It's cheesy, it skirts the question, and it isn't genuine. That's not what you're going for with this method either.

The best answer to the "weaknesses" question is a genuine one, but worded in a way that still demonstrates competence so that the interviewer feels comfortable hiring you. The same thing applies when it comes to your self-esteem: you should be honest with yourself about your weaknesses while also being fair and demonstrating that despite any weaknesses, you can still be good, likable, and capable.

As an example, maybe one of your weaknesses is that you have trouble making decisions. Your harsh inner critic might tell you that you're "paralyzed by decisions" or "can't make a decision to save your life," but I certainly hope you wouldn't say that in a job interview if you wanted to get a job offer. You may as well wear a shirt that says, "Please don't hire me, there are better options." The interviewer won't have much confidence in you, and you won't have much confidence in yourself either if you use this kind of language.

If you really wanted the job, imagine how you would genuinely convey the weakness of being indecisive to an interviewer. Maybe you'd say, "I'm very meticulous when it comes to decisions because I always want to make the best choice possible. Sometimes making decisions can be difficult for me, but I'm learning how to prioritize so I can make decisions more confidently." With an answer like that, you'd really impress the interviewer. This answer contains a few important components.

- **First, your assessment is reasonable.** You didn't use harsh words or labels, which shows that your weaknesses don't diminish your confidence in your abilities.
- **Second, it gave some helpful context.** This made the weakness seem more reasonable and didn't leave much room for judgment.
- **Finally, it demonstrates a growth mindset.** It shows that you want to grow and make progress, and this weakness won't hold you back from attaining your goals.

If imagining yourself in a job interview helps you conceptualize your weaknesses more fairly, then do whatever you need to do to get yourself into that mindset. Pretend you're preparing for an interview question by going through your list of weaknesses from earlier in the chapter. Develop an honest and confident conceptualization about the things you'd like to improve about yourself. It's usually very helpful to frame them not as traits you're ashamed of, but instead as weaknesses that don't hold you back.

7. Consider Whether a Weakness Could Be a Strength

You may not have considered it, but what if some of your perceived weaknesses are just strengths with really bad PR? Many people with low self-esteem have a real talent for twisting their positive traits and accomplishments so much that they sound mediocre or even shameful. Maybe you're doing that too.

In chapter 4, I asked you to pretend someone else was arguing that your positive traits were actually negative ones. Here, I want you to do the same thing, except now you're trying to argue that your negative traits aren't actually bad. For each of your "negative traits," ask yourself this question: What would the world be like if nobody possessed this trait? You may find, contrary to your initial perception, that the world may in some way be *worse* off if this trait didn't exist. For example, if you think of yourself as "weird," imagine what the world would be like without "weird" people. Everyone would be the same, conforming to a set of rigid expectations. There would be no challenge to the status quo, no questioning of norms, no significant social change. When you look at it this way, is it really such a bad thing to be weird?

It may not be obvious right away that some of your weaknesses are just strengths in disguise. Sometimes pejorative language can put a negative spin on positive traits. For example, the word "bossy" is often used to make assertiveness sound like a bad thing. Don't get me wrong, there's a clear difference between assertiveness and bossiness, but sometimes real and healthy assertiveness is incorrectly labeled as bossiness. Is there a more positive way to rethink some of your weaknesses? And is that positive phrasing actually more accurate?

Here are some examples of how strengths can masquerade as weaknesses:

> Weird → Unique
>
> Bossy → Assertive
>
> Overly sensitive → Emotionally aware and empathetic
>
> Argumentative → Strong critical thinking skills
>
> Bad at planning → Spontaneous
>
> Poor focus → Ability to multitask and think outside the box

Obviously, this method won't apply to all your weaknesses, and it's not meant to. Remember, self-esteem isn't about having no weaknesses, nor is it about turning your weaknesses into strengths. Of course, after working through this section, there will still be plenty of weaknesses that are plain and simply negative, no matter how you spin them. That's okay. But maybe some qualities you originally thought were weaknesses turned out to be just really good examples of the way your warped self-concept makes you seem much less capable or likable than you actually are. *That's* the point of this section—making sure you're being absolutely fair in your assessment of yourself. Like I said before, some people with low self-esteem have a real talent for twisting their traits to seem much worse than they are. Do you?

To Improve or Not to Improve . . .

Self-improvement is a very common approach to building self-esteem. After all, at face value, it makes sense. Common sense suggests that if your self-concept is overtaken by your weaknesses or deficits, then you can improve your self-esteem by improving on your weaknesses. However, even though this approach seems intuitive, there are several reasons it doesn't work.

For one, since low self-esteem is the result of a warped self-concept, it's very difficult, if not impossible, to change yourself enough that you *like* the warped reflection you see in your fun-house mirror. Your perception is the problem, not you. Since self-esteem isn't about who you are but about who you *think* you are, trying to change who you are doesn't change the mechanisms that caused your low self-esteem in the first place. That's why people with low self-esteem often feel inadequate even despite their best efforts. According to their warped self-concept and unfair standards, nothing they do will ever be good enough.

Second, there's no guarantee that any particular weakness will ever go away. You might struggle with it for the rest of your life. We all have weaknesses we just can't seem to overcome. Therefore, your self-acceptance shouldn't hinge on the severity or combination of your weaknesses. No human has ever lacked flaws, and you're no exception.

Third, it's common for people with low self-esteem to feel that nothing they ever do is good enough. They often use "good enough" as a benchmark for self-acceptance, striving for a vague and elusive goalpost that always seems just out of reach. This just keeps them feeling inadequate because they'll never really get there. Not only that, "good enough" also implies a state of contentment, where growth and improvement are no longer necessary. Anyone who values progress will have a hard time reaching this arbitrary level of achievement. Since humans are imperfect, we will always have more opportunity for improvement, so striving to reach "good enough" status implies that "good enough" is somewhere just beyond our current state. Of course, when you achieve some form of improvement, you may be bewildered to find that your original "good enough" benchmark rose along with it. While it's commendable to constantly raise the bar in response to personal growth, when the "good enough" threshold rises too, you'll never measure up.

Finally, attempting to improve your self-esteem by improving on your weaknesses comes with the risk of inadvertently reinforcing the idea that in order to like yourself you can't have weaknesses. When you have low self-esteem, it's easy to trick yourself into believing that in order to actually like and accept yourself you have to be perfect. To the contrary, self-esteem is all about allowing yourself to be imperfect and accepting yourself in spite of that. You don't need to measure up to any standard to have self-esteem; you just need to see the good that already exists in you.

The desire to improve is virtuous, and for some people, it's a core part of their value system. By no means is improving on weaknesses inherently detrimental to your self-esteem. In fact, it can have a positive impact on how you think of yourself. Improving on your weaknesses can demonstrate capability, which is a core part of your self-evaluation. But if you're not careful, constantly striving to improve can reinforce the same mechanisms that caused your warped self-concept in the first place. Self-esteem shouldn't be determined by whether or how much you improve on your negative character traits. The key distinction between whether self-improvement facilitates or hinders building self-esteem is the intention behind it. Are you striving to improve for its own sake, or out of a need to measure up?

Ultimately, the decision to work toward improving on your weaknesses or accepting yourself in spite of them is entirely up to you. I simply ask that you carefully consider how doing so might affect your self-esteem.

Self-Compassion Exercise:
Rethinking Your Weaknesses

Now's the time to apply everything you learned in this chapter. In the spaces on the next page, rewrite your weaknesses using one or more of the methods you learned in this chapter. Use your discretion and intuition to determine which method(s) to use for each of your negative traits. There's no "right" way to do this exercise, so there's no need to strive for perfection. Self-compassion never needs to be perfect to be valuable.

For your reference, here's a list of the seven methods we covered:
1. Be Specific
2. No Name-Calling
3. Understand How You Compensate for Your Weaknesses
4. Avoid Universals
5. State It as an Opinion, Not a Fact
6. Use the Job Interview Technique
7. Consider Whether a Weakness Could Be a Strength

To download a free copy of this worksheet, visit rethinkyourself.info/worksheets or scan the QR code in the back of the book.

Weakness: _____

Reframe: _____

Weakness: _____

Reframe: _____

Weakness: _____

Reframe: _____

Weakness: _____

Reframe: _____

Weakness: _____

Reframe: _____

Weakness: _____

Reframe: _____

Weakness: _____

Reframe: _____

Weakness: _____

Reframe: _____

Weakness: _____

Reframe: _____

Weakness: _____

Reframe: _____

Accepting Yourself Anyway

Now that you've conceptualized your weaknesses more fairly, you still have to accept yourself in spite of them. Before you move on to the next chapter, take some time to build tolerance of your weaknesses. Your level of tolerance for your weaknesses has a direct impact on your self-esteem. So anytime one of your weaknesses comes to mind, show your harsh inner critic you can tolerate it. You might find it helpful to tack a short statement onto the end of your reframed weaknesses to promote self-acceptance Here are a few examples:

> ". . . and that's okay."
>
> ". . . but that doesn't diminish my value."
>
> ". . . but everyone has weaknesses."
>
> ". . . but it doesn't define me."
>
> ". . . so what?"

You can use one of these statements or make your own. Reflect on your self-compassionate statement until you feel that your weaknesses are no longer barriers to a strong self-esteem. It takes time, so be patient.

Remember, it's okay to have weaknesses. You don't need to ignore them and you don't need to make them positive. You just need to make sure that the way you think about them is realistic, and that you don't let them define you.

Chapter 12

"Feeling" Good About Yourself

As a therapist, I talk about emotions all day. Difficult or unwanted emotions are a huge part of why most people decide to go to therapy. These emotions can feel out of control, annoying, embarrassing, confusing, scary, paralyzing, inconvenient, and all kinds of other things. But as uncomfortable as they may feel, it's imperative that you learn to accept them.

Most books on self-esteem leave out the topic of emotional acceptance, but emotional acceptance is an important component of self-acceptance. Emotions are one of the most integral and personal aspects of our humanity. They're a deep, personal, and genuine piece of who we all are. They're highly individual, and they reveal what matters to us. They're gateways into our pain and triumph, the memories we hold dear, our regrets, our values, and more. But like it or not, our emotions are a reality we can't ignore. Take it from a therapist—there is no "hack" to make your emotions go away. Unless you want to fight them for the rest of your life, you'll have to make peace with them somehow. And if you want to build your self-esteem, you have to learn to accept all parts of yourself, including *and especially* your emotions.

Emotional acceptance can be difficult if your emotions have historically been a source of self-criticism, or even ridicule or judgment from others. There's an implicit understanding in our culture that if we can't "control" our emotions that means we're weak. But we're also wrongfully taught that controlling our emotions means suppressing or denying them. And that's the opposite of acceptance. Your emotions are not shameful; they're an essential component of what makes you you.

We all have different relationships to our emotions. Some people experience and express their emotions willingly. They feel their emotions strongly and don't shy away from them, either because they're unable, unwilling, or both. These people will probably have an easier time completing this chapter. They may find it interesting and revelatory. Some people, on the other hand, will do everything in their power not to feel or express their emotions. They fear their emotions or are embarrassed by them. They were never equipped with skills to regulate their emotions in their formative years, so out of necessity, they've expertly developed methods to suppress or avoid them. These people will have a different experience with this chapter. Whatever your current relationship to your emotions, recognize that there's no shame in where you are now. You're reading this book to learn and grow, and in the end you'll be better off for it.

It's important to note, before beginning, that this chapter won't directly focus on emotion-regulation techniques but instead on *accepting* your emotions. Even though acceptance can be an effective way to cope with emotions, it's not the be-all and end-all approach, so it's not always the best way to cope. This chapter can be used in conjunction with other coping techniques from therapy or other self-help books, but it's not intended to be a replacement for these techniques.

Emotions vs. Mental Disorders

To avoid any misunderstanding, it's important to note the difference between an emotion and a mental disorder. Emotions are usually transient and tend to come and go. They happen to everyone and don't usually cause lasting distress. A mental disorder is when these emotions (and other symptoms) cause significant distress and/or functional impairment. For example, sadness is an emotion, but depression is a mental disorder. This chapter is about transient emotions, not about mental disorders. Struggles with chronic or significantly distressing emotions might warrant more support on emotion regulation than this chapter can provide. If you've been diagnosed with or suspect that you might have a mental disorder, I encourage you to seek care from a licensed therapist.

"Feeling" Good About Yourself

Emotional Acceptance

Acceptance can mean a lot of things. In chapter 10, acceptance meant accepting uncertainty rather than trying to give yourself a sense of false certainty to avoid the discomfort of not knowing. It didn't mean *approving* of the uncertainty, but simply letting go of fruitless attempts to subvert it. When it comes to emotional acceptance, you've certainly got to start by acknowledging that your emotions exist, because you won't get anywhere by ignoring them. But emotional acceptance means a little more than that. Emotional acceptance is a component of self-acceptance, and that type of acceptance means welcoming or regarding with approval (even though you're not perfect). The same goes for your emotions.

To get started, be willing to allow your emotions to exist as they are; don't force them to be what you want them to be or think they should be. That can feel unpleasant, scary, or overwhelming. It can go against what you were taught. But you can never appreciate something while you're also trying to make it something it's not. When I start treatment with a new client, after gathering information about their reasons for seeking therapy, we develop a list of goals to guide our work together. A goal I hear a lot is "I want to learn how to control my emotions." Whenever I hear this, I know I have to break the truth to them: that's not really possible. Therapy can be highly effective at reducing the frequency, duration, and severity of unhelpful emotions over the long-term, but getting there involves *tolerating* emotions, not *controlling* them. Unfortunately, we just can't control our emotions in the way we hope to. I know, emotions can be inconvenient, but therapy and general self-improvement aren't necessarily about what's convenient—they're about what's healthy.

The desire to control emotions often stems from a lack of acceptance of them and, more foundationally, a misunderstanding about how emotions work. When someone tries to "control" their emotions, what they're actually doing is suppressing or avoiding them. As much as we may want to suppress our emotions, doing that isn't really the best approach. And there are two important reasons for that.

We Can't Just Make Our Negative Emotions Go Away

What's the worst thing you can say to someone who is angry or anxious? *Just calm down.* This statement is more likely to fan the flames of wrath or panic than extinguish them. That's because emotions rarely (if ever) do what we tell

169

them. They're not like a dog that just completed obedience training; they're stubborn. In fact, when we fight our emotions, they usually fight right back.

Our emotions demand to be felt, one way or another. When an emotion pops up and you try to suppress or avoid it, you don't really make it go away. It still exists, even if you're not giving it your attention. And it may end up affecting you in ways you don't even realize. Avoiding your feelings is like playing roulette with them: you risk them coming back up later when you're not prepared for them. Instead, there are ways to address your feelings on your own watch. You can address them as they come, or file them away for later when you have the time or capacity to deal with them (like in therapy or while journaling), just as long as you tend to them eventually. Emotional health isn't about suppressing your feelings, it's about managing them effectively.

What If I Don't Feel Certain Emotions?

While you may experience some emotions less frequently than others, it's unlikely that you don't experience them at all. Everyone experiences emotions. Some people are simply more aware of their emotions than others. If certain emotions feel unfamiliar, it could be that you've gotten so used to suppressing them that you don't even recognize when they come up. For example, when someone isn't in tune with their anxiety, they might experience worry as fatigue, difficulty sleeping, irritability, or gastrointestinal distress. It's not that they're immune to anxiety, it's that they aren't aware they're feeling anxious. If you have difficulty identifying your emotions, it might be helpful to see a licensed therapist if you have access to care. You could also seek deeper understanding by reading a self-help book specifically about emotional awareness.

Suppressing your emotions is a form of self-rejection because it means there's a piece of yourself you're not willing to accept. Learning to accept all parts of yourself, even the parts you don't like, is key to building a strong self-esteem. And while you may not like your negative emotions, that doesn't mean they're a sign of weakness. Trust me, everyone has emotions they don't like; some people are just really good at hiding them. Emotions are a reality we simply can't deny. They don't make us weak, they make us human.

It's Unhealthy to Shut Out Negative Emotions

A common misconception about mental health is that happiness is the absence of negative emotions. The academic research on emotions says otherwise. Jordi Quoidbach and his colleagues[1] coined the term *emodiversity* to refer to the diversity of emotions, both positive and negative, that a person experiences in a given period of time.

Although we often assume it's best to experience mostly positive emotions, studies indicate something different. In fact, people with more emodiversity (i.e., more diverse and complex emotional experiences) are often more resilient to adversity than those who experience fewer, or even mostly positive, emotions.[2] Why do you think therapists so often emphasize the importance of feeling your emotions?

Emodiversity is a lot like biodiversity. The greater the diversity of species in an ecosystem, the more the ecosystem thrives, even if that means many of the species are hunted or must compete for limited resources. In a similar way, it's important that we all experience a diversity of emotions in order to keep our psychological ecosystem thriving, even if at times the negative emotions seem to compete with the positive ones.

We're more likely to thrive when we have a rich and complex emotional life. Our negative emotions help us identify problems, form social bonds and norms, and develop a strong value system. Our emotions largely represent our ability to care. But it's hard to know for sure whether the emotions themselves are responsible for the benefits shown in studies on emodiversity, or whether emotional self-awareness is. After all, experiencing a range of emotions is the norm, not the exception. It could be that emotionally self-aware people don't necessarily feel more emotions but are better able to identify and articulate their emotions in studies. And that could explain why studies on emodiversity reach the conclusions they do.

Our emotions can only help us if we let them, which makes sense when you think about it. When we're attuned to our emotions, we can allow them to supplement our rational decision-making process rather than override it. When we ignore our negative emotions, we're unaware of how they impact our perception, so we can't account for them. They might influence our thought processes in ways we don't even realize. When we become detached from our own emotions, we have a hard time even distinguishing them from logic and reasoning. Our emotions have a job to do, but we need to supervise them. Otherwise, they do a job they were never equipped to do, which can have consequences on our mental health and our view of who we are.

Understanding the Purpose of Your Feelings

Allowing your emotions to exist is only half the battle. Emotional acceptance is more than just acknowledging that your emotions exist; it also involves viewing them favorably. Of course, it's a lot easier to think of positive emotions favorably. After all, they're positive! It's the negative ones you'll need to focus on most in this chapter. Keep in mind that accepting is not the same as expressing. It's up to you to decide whether or how to express your emotions based on the unique circumstances of a given situation. What matters for your self-esteem is that your negative emotions are not a source of self-criticism.

Accepting your negative emotions is an especially complicated feat if you've been taught that emotions are shameful or make you weak. If that was your experience, you'll need to unlearn a few things about your emotions in the process. A good place to start is by seeking an accurate and compassionate understanding of what your emotions do for you. When it comes to emotions, a profoundly effective way to understand their purpose is to imagine that you're completely incapable of feeling them. I've used this thought experiment many times in this book, so it's clear just how effective it is at illuminating the value of something. Here's an example to show how to apply the thought experiment to emotions:

Imagine that someone you love just got fired or laid off from their job. They're worried about how they'll pay their bills or put food on the table. They wonder how they'll find another good-paying job in time. They're feeling hopeless. Since you care about this person, you might feel a bit saddened by the bad news as well. In response, you'd offer to support them in any way you can. Maybe you'd pay for their groceries for a week, or sit with them and allow them to talk through their feelings with you. Essentially, you'd experience empathy. You'd be able to connect their emotions to similar emotions you've experienced in the past, and this gives you the ability to respond to their emotional needs.

Now imagine this same situation, but instead imagine that you're incapable of feeling sadness. Your friend would express their feelings to you, and you wouldn't feel much in response. You'd assume they'll be okay, or maybe you'd even have difficulty understanding their perspective. You wouldn't be able to validate them or support them. To look at this from another angle, you could even imagine that your friend is the one who's incapable of feeling sadness. If they seem to have it all together and are assuring you they're okay, you might be reluctant to offer support. You wouldn't want to bother them or project your own feelings onto them. They might actually be in trouble if they don't receive whatever support their friends are willing to offer, but by not feeling sad, there isn't much for their friends to empathize with.

By imagining a situation where sadness doesn't exist, it's easy to see that the role of sadness is to make empathy possible; it allows us to form strong bonds with others and ensures our needs are met. Even though we consider sadness a negative emotion, it serves a purpose, and it's clear in this example that the benefits sadness offers (empathy, connection, support) outweigh the drawback (emotional discomfort). That doesn't mean you need to be overcome with sadness to receive its benefit. Even a tinge of sadness, or any other emotion, can often be enough.

Here's another example to show the role of negative emotions. Suppose there's a hurricane headed toward your city, and forecasts are showing that it's strong enough to do a lot of damage. Naturally you'd feel a bit (or very) worried about what could happen. Because of your anxiety about the storm, you'd feel compelled to take some precautions to ensure your safety. You might evacuate to somewhere safer. You might assemble some safety supplies or create an emergency plan. You'd probably take necessary steps to secure your home in any way you can. And all of this preparation was in response to your feeling of anxiety.

Now suppose the same thing happens, but you're incapable of feeling worried. Maybe you'd assume everything will be fine, and there's no reason to do anything to prepare for the hurricane. You'd lack the capacity to foresee possible threats, and without that capacity, you wouldn't be able to prepare for a genuine emergency. Your safety would be at risk.

By removing emotion from the situation, it becomes clear how worry and anxiety function to help you avoid danger. Anxiety's job is to alert you when something might be awry. It ensures you act quickly and decisively so that you and those you care about remain safe.

You can use this process to reveal the purpose of any negative emotion, not just sadness and anxiety. In fact, we used this process to understand guilt in chapter 7. Even though guilt is an unpleasant emotion, it's far from bad! It's amazing how something that feels so pesky can suddenly seem so important when you imagine it not being there. See the following table for suggestions on the purposes of many common negative emotions. Note that shame is not represented in the table because shame has no benefits.

What Does This Emotion Offer Me?

Anger → Serves as a barometer for fairness and justice

Anxiety/Worry → Alerts us to potential threats

Boredom → Encourages us to seek stimulation and pleasure

Confusion → Encourages us to search for answers and find solutions

Disgust → Encourages us to avoid or renounce contamination, embarrassment, or injustice

Embarrassment → Helps us maintain a positive reputation by avoiding situations that might lead to ridicule

Fear → Alerts us to danger

Guilt → Ensures we remain accountable to our values

Jealousy → Allows us to identify, evaluate, and address the aspects of our lives that we feel dissatisfied with

Overwhelm → Reminds us to take a break to preserve our well-being

Sadness → Gives us capacity for empathy and connection

Now, I acknowledge that I presented this idea in a nice, clean package. I made negative emotions seem so much simpler and more straightforward than they actually are. In each example, the corresponding emotion was the most rational response for the situation. But what about situations where the emotion doesn't seem appropriate? For example, you may experience anxiety at the dentist or while speaking in front of a crowd, neither of which represents any real danger. Or maybe you feel anger in traffic, despite no real injustice or mistreatment occurring. These and many other scenarios are times when an emotional reaction isn't really necessary or helpful. How can we accept our emotions in times like these?

In short, our emotions, like us, aren't perfect. Sometimes they get it wrong. Sometimes they don't know the difference between threat or mistreatment and typical mundane occurrences. Even though our emotions are supposed to help, they don't always succeed. But just like you, your emotions don't need to be perfect in order for you to accept them.

Keep in mind that your emotions aren't responsible for your circumstances. For example, when you feel lonely, your emotions are encouraging you to seek companionship and connection. However, these things aren't always readily available, for any number of reasons. That doesn't mean your feeling of loneliness was wrong, just that the circumstances aren't conducive to meeting the need your loneliness alerted you to. When you experience fear, that emotion is still trying to help you, even if the thing that triggered it didn't turn out to be as threatening as you initially perceived it to be. In other words, your emotions are always valid, even when they don't seem to provide any real benefit in a given situation. But more on that in a bit.

Emotions as Acts of Self-Worth

In chapter 2, you learned that acts of self-worth are efforts you make to pursue, honor, or reinforce your intrinsic human needs; and that you engage in acts of self-worth all the time, probably without even realizing it. Emotional responses to certain situations can also be considered acts of self-worth. Consider the value these emotional reactions might have by honoring your inherent worth:

You become angry after being disrespected.

You feel disappointed when a date cancels.

You feel hurt when you find out a loved one lied to you.

You're annoyed when someone oversteps one of your boundaries.

These are all normal emotional reactions to their corresponding circumstances. They're also confirmation that you're worthy of your intrinsic needs. Imagine what it would mean if you couldn't experience an appropriate emotional reaction to being disrespected or lied to. You'd allow others to walk all over you, mistreat you, or take advantage of you. Essentially, you would deny your intrinsic needs. Instead, when you experience an emotional reaction to mistreatment, unmet expectations, or other negative experiences, you are (maybe without even realizing it) acknowledging that you deserve better. After all, why would you react that way if your needs didn't matter?

Ideally, after experiencing these situations, you'd feel compelled to do whatever is necessary to make sure your intrinsic needs are met. Maybe you'd let your friend or loved one know they hurt you and you expect better, or you'd reevaluate whether your relationships are good for you. But even just feeling negatively after a negative experience proves that you know the experience invalidated your innate worth.

Viewing your negative emotions as reflections of your self-worth is just another way of understanding the purpose and value of those emotions in your day-to-day life. Your negative emotions aren't a bad thing, even though they're uncomfortable or painful.

Thanking Your Negative Emotions

Now here's an idea that might sound pretty outlandish at first: Have you ever considered thanking your negative emotions? While it may sound odd or even counterintuitive, this technique isn't uncommon in therapy. Not only does thanking your emotions help you more effectively manage them, but it also helps you treat yourself with more compassion, since your emotions are an important part of who you are. When you treat your emotions with compassion, by extension, you're treating yourself with compassion as well.

To explain the logic behind thanking your emotions, I like to use this analogy. Imagine that you have a young child, say five or six years old, and they decided to help you by doing the dishes for you without being asked to. Now, children this young usually lack the skills to properly clean dishes, so their well-intentioned act of service was executed terribly. They've splashed water all over the kitchen, broken a few dishes, and the ones they did wash aren't even fully clean. They've made quite a mess for you. You could respond to the child in a number of ways: you could yell at them, telling them to never help you again; you could send them to their room because you just feel too overwhelmed to deal with them; or you could choose to be kind and thank them for trying to help (even though their act of kindness wasn't actually helpful). So what do you do?

While you may want to yell at the child out of justifiable anger, this response lacks compassion and is likely to cause your child to feel discouraged and unappreciated. Just like emotions, you can't simply revoke your child's free will, so yelling at them doesn't prevent any future mishaps; it only creates conflict and hostility when those mishaps inevitably arise in the future. You could instead send them to their room so you can deal with the mess on your own. But since you've banished them without including them in the cleanup, what's to stop them from making the same mistakes again and again? You haven't established a partnership with your child, so they'll just continue on with their usual ways because there's no reason for them to change. On the other hand, if you thank them for trying, you've chosen to address your child's actions directly and now have the opportunity to teach them how to do the dishes properly so that maybe next time their act of service will actually be helpful. By granting them compassion, you can help them improve because of it. The same applies to your emotions.

Emotions exist to help you. Even though they don't always offer real help, they're trying. I promise, their purpose isn't to torture you, even if it feels that way. Showing hostility toward the emotions that don't seem to be helpful on the surface is just another way of showing hostility to yourself. No matter how much distress your emotions cause you, it's not productive to make them out to be your enemy.

If you choose to embrace your emotions, thanking them is a great way to do it. Start by evaluating them to determine what they were *trying* to do for you. You can't validate or thank your emotions if you don't understand their intention. Try to avoid using a right/wrong mindset because validation isn't always about right or wrong. In the dishes analogy, your child did the dishes "wrong," but you can still appreciate their attempt at helping you. Understanding your emotions as they are is a lot more effective than judging how good/bad or right/wrong they are. And gaining this understanding doesn't require anything more than a quick internal reflection. Here are some examples:

You become angry when someone cuts in line at the grocery store. *"Thank you, anger, for alerting me to the unfairness of this situation, since I don't deserve to be disregarded."*

You feel nervous just before a big job interview. *"Thank you, anxiety, for reminding me how big this opportunity is and trying to keep me alert so I perform at my best."*

Expressing gratitude is the first part in thanking your negative emotions. Like in the dishes analogy, you also need to hold your emotions accountable. You're responsible for supervising your emotions by teaching them how to actually help you. You can follow up your expression of gratitude with an assertive "BUT." This is your opportunity to identify a more appropriate response to the situation, when applicable. For example:

> "Thank you, anger, for alerting me to unfairness, BUT I don't need to get too worked up about it, because I can easily rectify the situation by speaking up for myself."

> "Thank you, anxiety, for reminding me how big this opportunity is and trying to keep me alert so I perform at my best, BUT it's not the end of the world if I don't do well, and I will be okay."

Sometimes, your "BUT" statement after your expression of gratitude will point out that the emotion wasn't needed since it didn't offer any real help. Other times, it will call out your emotion for being out of proportion with the situation. Still other times, it will help you "zoom out" and see the bigger picture so that your emotion doesn't override your normal faculties. Whatever the situation, it's important that you show your emotion what an appropriate reaction to a situation is, just like you showed your child the right way to do the dishes in the analogy.

Ideally, the degree of your emotional reaction would be in proportion with the situation that caused it so that your response can be appropriate and effective, but that's not always the case. Whether your emotion was helpful or not, whether it was "too big" or just right, **the emotion was still valid. It was valid because it was real. It was valid because it impacted you. It was valid because there was a reason for it.** Your child's desire to help you was still valid even if they didn't accomplish the goal. The same is absolutely true for your emotions.

Thanking your emotions has two main purposes, each representing a component of the kind of acceptance you're aiming for here. The first purpose is to help you gain an understanding of your emotions so that you can show them (and yourself) some appreciation. Doing so encourages you to step outside your discomfort and acknowledge why you're feeling that emotion. The second purpose is to encourage you to allow your emotions to exist as they are, rather than suppressing or ignoring them. Freely experiencing your emotions is an important part of emotional well-being and, when done effectively, can help you respond to your emotions more rationally and calmly. If you can achieve emotional acceptance, then strong negative emotions won't be as much of a source of self-criticism.

Emotions vs. Actions

It's my firm and unwavering belief that emotions are valid in all circumstances, no matter what. Of course, many of my clients challenge this assertion, and most of the counter-arguments I hear wrongly conflate emotions with actions. It's very important to understand the difference, because while all emotions are valid, not all *expressions* of emotion are.

As an example, anger is an emotion while aggression refers to actions. Anger is something that is only felt internally. Aggression encompasses disrespectful actions including shouting, interrupting, threatening, and even physical violence. It's okay to experience anger as an emotion, but as soon as that anger is expressed as aggression, it's no longer simply an emotion but also an action. Often my clients tell me something like, "My anger wasn't justified. I got too angry and lashed out." I then have to remind them, "Your anger wasn't the problem, it was how you expressed it."

If you have trouble accepting and validating your emotions, be sure to distinguish them from actions. Emotions are never a choice, and we can't control them nearly as well as we think we can. We do have control over our actions, and while an action might be considered unacceptable, that doesn't mean the emotion that caused it was also unacceptable.

When Thanking Your Emotions Is Too Difficult

Sometimes it's clear what your emotions are trying to do for you, and sometimes it's not. This is especially true when you're new to this or don't have a therapist to help you work through your feelings. Your emotions always have a purpose, but that doesn't mean their purpose is always obvious. It's hard to know how to thank your emotions when they only seem to cause problems. Even when it's clear how your emotions are trying to help you, thanking them can be difficult. Sometimes your emotions are so painful, annoying, or overwhelming that you just don't have it in you to thank them. That's okay. You don't have to thank your emotions every single time. You do, however, have to resist the urge to suppress or avoid them. When you suppress your emotions, you reject a core part of yourself. So when thanking your emotions is too difficult, just say this instead:

"Hello, [emotion]."

You don't have to do anything beyond just acknowledging their presence. You don't always need to understand them, and you don't always need to appreciate them. Just be friendly toward them. Remember, your emotions are an extension of yourself; treat them like it.

When your instinct is to suppress or avoid your emotions, it's important that you instead acknowledge them. A friendly "hello" shows that you're not too ashamed to even look at your emotions. It means welcoming them in rather than shutting them out. You may not always understand your emotions, but you should never deny them.

Self-Compassion Exercise:
Thanking Your Emotions

Now that you have a framework for allowing and accepting your emotions, you can put it into practice. When you experience emotional distress, take a moment to seek a compassionate understanding of the purpose it intended to fulfill for you. Remember, it isn't about right/wrong or good/bad. Once you have a compassionate understanding, validate your emotional experience by thanking it for doing its job (or trying to). Then feel free to call out or challenge your emotion if it wasn't needed in a given situation or was out of proportion.

While it's important to allow your emotions to exist, you don't always have to engage with or express your emotions immediately as they arise. Certain circumstances make it difficult or inconvenient to tend to your emotions, such as during important meetings, tests, or other obligations. In these circumstances, it's okay to compartmentalize the emotion and save it for later, *as long as you give the emotion your attention when you are able.*

Although thanking your emotions is an entirely internal process, you might find it easier to think objectively about your emotions if you write them down. Use the spaces on the next page to journal your emotions and work through the process systematically, if you'd like, though writing them down isn't necessary.

To download a free copy of this worksheet, visit rethinkyourself.info/worksheets or scan the QR code in the back of the book.

Situation:

_____

Emotion: _____
What if this emotion didn't exist?

_____

What can I infer about the purpose of this emotion?

_____

Thank you:

_____

BUT:

_____

Remember, if it's too hard to thank your emotions, just welcome them in with a friendly hello.

Situation:

_____

Emotion: _____
What if this emotion didn't exist?

_____

What can I infer about the purpose of this emotion?

_____

Thank you:

_____

BUT:

_____

Remember, if it's too hard to thank your emotions, just welcome them in with a friendly hello.

Conclusion

Congratulations on completing this book! It took a lot of hard work, and some parts were probably pretty challenging or uncomfortable, but hopefully your self-esteem is in a much better place now than when you started. Even though you've completed all the exercises, you haven't definitively "conquered" low self-esteem. That's because you're never done building self-esteem, just like you're never done learning or growing or making healthy choices. You've finished the hard work of building your self-esteem, so now your main task is maintaining it.

In life, you may experience periods of success or failure, growth or stagnation, pleasure or pain. You may notice your self-esteem waning and waxing with the seasons of your life. Sometimes you may need to take extra care to protect your self-esteem, and other times, self-esteem may just feel natural. After you've made progress in any area of your life, it's normal to sometimes experience some regression afterward. That's not a cause for concern; it's just an indication that you need to put in a little more work.

This book is a tool, so you can use it whenever you need it. Just because you used it once doesn't mean you can't use it again. When you need a booster or refresher, feel free to revisit any chapters you think you might need to brush up on. You might even want to take some time right now to go back to any chapters you found more challenging. There might be a little more work for you to do in those areas.

When you began this book, you may have assumed that building your self-esteem meant ignoring and shutting out your inner critic. That's usually how it's presented at least. But as you now know, your inner critic isn't all bad. In fact, its job is to help you, even if it's not always good at doing its job. *Your job isn't to fight your inner critic but to foster its development.*

You now know the difference between legitimate and harsh self-criticism and how to respond most effectively to each. When you experience legitimate self-criticism, even though it's uncomfortable, you should try to listen to what it's telling you. It's only trying to hold you accountable.

When you experience harsh self-criticism, you now have an arsenal of approaches to take in response to it. You could honor your worthiness of respect by rebuking your inner critic's disrespectful words and tone. You could remind yourself where this thought may be coming from and use cognitive defusion to separate the thought from your reality. You could reframe shame-based language to sound more like guilt, then be accountable for your actions. You could use mutual validation to make your inner critic work for you rather than against you. You could practice the Three Cons of mistakes to let go of any unnecessary self-blame. Or you could practice accepting uncertainty if there's no evidence that you actually did anything wrong.

An important part of maintaining your self-esteem is giving yourself credit where it's due. That means acknowledging your positive qualities and celebrating your successes. It won't make you arrogant to acknowledge what you like about yourself, and you don't have to be perfect or the best in order to do that. Everyone brings something to the table, including you.

Through all of this, your self-worth gives you reason to put in the effort. No matter how you feel about yourself, you have value. You are worthy of happiness, compassion, love, health, and so much more. And importantly, you're worthy of self-esteem. You'll never give yourself the things you need unless you understand that you're worthy of them. You don't need to earn them, but you do need to pursue them. And now, you will.

Appendix: Self-Advocacy 101

Five Basic Assertiveness Techniques

Assertiveness is an essential component of both building confidence and honoring your self-worth. Take a closer look at your intrinsic human needs from chapter 2 and you'll find that communication and advocacy play a role in all of them. You simply cannot honor your innate worth without them. And while learning how to be assertive isn't necessarily a step in "rethinking yourself," it's hard to leave it out of the discussion of self-esteem entirely. This appendix is included as supplementary information to build on the self-esteem you developed throughout the book.

This appendix covers five basic assertiveness techniques. Most of them use a script or outline, which makes them easy to remember. That's important because accessing rational and objective thought in times of conflict or vulnerability can be especially difficult. Having a script or outline prepared ahead of time alleviates the pressure to come up with a clear and effective message on the spot.

If you're not great at memorizing (like me) or you're afraid of coming across as robotic, scripts might not be your thing. Keep reading, because at the end of the appendix, I'll deconstruct all of the techniques to help you build an intuitive understanding of them. Even if you don't follow them to the letter, you can still use the spirit of each technique in your communication.

Technique #1: "I" Statements

"I" statements are one of the most widely known assertiveness techniques, probably because they have broad applicability. They teach us how to frame our statements by both taking ownership over our feelings and avoiding accusatory or inflammatory language. "I" statements follow a specific script that keeps the focus of the statement on yourself. Here's the general outline:

"I feel _____ when you _____ because _____ ."

Below are some examples:

> "I feel self-conscious when you make comments about my body because I'm insecure about my appearance."
>
> "I feel violated when you enter my bedroom without my permission because my privacy is important to me."
>
> "I feel anxious when you don't respond to my texts because it makes me doubt what I say."

"I" statements are effective because focusing on your feelings rather than the other person's actions reduces the odds that they'll react defensively. Think of it this way: the opposite of an "I" statement is a "you" statement, which would sound something like this:

> "You frustrate me when you arrive late because it's rude."
>
> "You don't listen to me and that makes you a bad partner."

This type of statement directs all the focus (and blame) onto the listener, who, instinctively, will likely feel the need to defend themselves rather than listen openly. While "I" statements (and all other assertiveness techniques) don't guarantee that potential arguments will be diverted, the first-person language is meant to reduce the chances of conflict by communicating clearly and non-aggressively.

"You" statements can be sneaky because they can sometimes look a lot like "I" statements on the surface. Be careful not to inadvertently point proverbial fingers when you make statements like these:

> "I feel like you're being unreasonable."

> "I feel upset by how stubborn you're being."

These statements may look like "I" statements at first, but ultimately they mostly focus on the other person. They make accusations about the other person rather than helping you take ownership over your perspective.

Be careful not to make assumptions or use generalizations or labels. That's more likely to cause the other person to feel defensive, which closes them off to listening to you. Here are some examples of generalizations that limit the effectiveness of "I" statements.

> "I feel embarrassed when you're *disrespectful* to my friend."

> "I feel frustrated when you *always* dismiss my opinions because *it seems like* you don't respect my views."

Make sure you only focus on a singular behavior or issue. Avoid words like "always" or "never" because they're usually exaggerations and therefore unfair. Also try to be as specific as possible. Speak about specific behaviors rather than clusters of behaviors. In the example above, what behaviors might have come across as disrespectful? Make sure to name and focus on those.

"I" statements require insight, which is partly why they're so effective. To use them effectively, you have to identify, evaluate, and articulate what you're feeling, which doesn't usually happen automatically. This technique forces you to stop for a minute and think about what you're feeling and why. Generally, the more insightful you are about what's happening in your head, the more accurate, rational, and respectful you'll be in communicating about it.

Although "I" statements are a helpful way to express your feelings, they aren't as applicable to other situations, like responding to resistance, communicating disagreement, or making requests. That's what other techniques are for.

Technique #2: "I Think, I Feel, I Want"

"I think, I feel, I want" is a way to assertively ask someone for something, such as a change in their behavior or their help with a task. As you may have noticed from the title, this technique consists of three basic sentences to structure your request in a way that's clear and effective: I think . . . I feel . . . I want . . . However, your sentences don't have to start with these exact phrases, as long as they address each part adequately.

I think . . .

The first step in using this technique is to establish your assessment. What have you observed? Why is this request important? Sometimes this will involve an objective and observable fact. Other times you'll acknowledge your perception, which may be different from the perception of others. When that's the case, remember that your perspective on a situation is subjective, so don't present your viewpoint as a fact. You might find it helpful to preface your statement with a softening phrase such as "I see" or "It seems like." Not only does framing the statement this way sound less inflammatory, but it also keeps you open to the possibility that you could simply be misunderstanding. Remember, your first sentence doesn't necessarily have to begin with the words "I think." Here are some examples:

> "I see that you've been giving me lots of reminders about the upcoming deadline."
>
> "Lately it seems like you've been spending less time with me."

It's important that this statement doesn't include any judgments, assumptions, or attacks. It's simply an observation, not a determination of good or bad, right or wrong. You can address how the observation affects you in the next step.

I feel . . .

Now's your chance to explain how the observation makes you feel. It's important to communicate this point clearly, because it tells the other person why this issue matters. Just like with the "I think" statements, this sentence doesn't need to start with the words, "I feel." No matter how you frame your statement, make sure to take full ownership over your feelings. Avoid "you" statements! Here are some examples of "I feel" statements that follow the "I think" statements above:

> "It causes me to doubt myself more."
>
> "It worries me that your opinion of me may have changed."

Though this statement will often communicate an emotion, it doesn't have to. Some situations don't necessarily have an emotional impact, but they still matter. That's when you can communicate a tangible impact the situation is having on you. Here are some examples of statements that communicate a tangible impact:

> "It creates more work for me."
>
> "It caused me to miss my deadline."
>
> "It created a lot of confusion and ambiguity."

The main point of this step is to simply communicate how the situation impacted you. That encourages the other person to listen to your statements with openness and empathy, *as long as you avoid inflammatory or accusatory language.*

I want . . .

Now that you've addressed what's happening, you can make your request. You've already shown that this is a real problem with real impacts, so your request is already valid. Whatever you ask of the other person, it should ideally meet the following criteria:

- **Your request should be specific.** You can't ask for something general like "try harder" or "be nicer." Not only do generalized requests feel more inflammatory to the other person, but they also make it harder for you to determine whether the other person complied.
- **Your request should address a behavioral issue.** You can't ask someone to change their feelings, attitude, or opinions. Everyone is entitled

to their own thoughts, but their behaviors are what impact others. Try to focus on what they're doing (or not doing).

- **Your request should be positive whenever possible.** This simply means that you should ask for what you *want*, not what you want to stop. For example, instead of asking someone to stop sending you text messages while you're at work, you could ask them to wait until your shift is over.

However, there are bound to be exceptions. You don't need to treat these criteria like laws if you genuinely feel an exception is necessary. Use your intuition and trust your gut.

Here are some examples of "I want" statements that follow the "I think" and "I feel" statements that preceded them:

> "Can you please make an effort to be on time to things so that I don't have to wait each time?"
>
> "Can you please allow me the freedom to manage tasks on my own?"
>
> "Can you please tell me if I've done something wrong?"

"I think, I feel, I want" is a helpful way to frame requests by making a comprehensive yet concise case for why your request is important and deserving of attention. It encourages the other person to be more open and less defensive. It's a way to ensure your needs are addressed, but in a way that's polite and respectful to all involved.

Technique #3: Mutual Validation

You should be familiar with this one by now—it's the technique you used to respond to your inner critic in chapter 8. Mutual validation helps you stand your ground in the face of opposing viewpoints, which is particularly difficult if you're not used to assertiveness. Maybe you've had experiences of simply giving in to others because you just don't have it in you to go against the grain. When opposition arises, mutual validation is exactly what you need.

As you know, mutual validation helps you highlight the validity of two opinions or perspectives that have few points of intersection so that the people who hold each of these viewpoints can develop respect and understanding and, if necessary, make a compromise. It's about finding even a kernel of truth in the other person's statement, even if you don't fully agree with them. That requires you to try to understand the other person's perspective, preferences, needs, or motivation.

Don't jump to the validating part right away, though. You may need to do some preparation first. Start by making sure you have a strong and accurate understanding of the opposing viewpoint. If you speak without a proper understanding, you might sound more aggressive than you intend. Ask yourself, Would I be able to make a strong argument in their defense? If you can't answer yes to this question, you might need to ask more questions before addressing any of their points. In exploring their perspective, you might find that you initially misunderstood their points, and that there's more common ground than you initially thought. But that doesn't necessarily mean the goal of validating the other person is to reach full agreement. Instead, the goal is for you to acknowledge that, at least from a certain angle (which usually isn't the same as your own), the other person's perspective makes sense. Once you can do that, then you can begin to validate their perspective. Here are some examples of validating statements:

> "I can see why you think that."
>
> "That makes sense."
>
> "I understand why (then explain their point so they know you get it)."
>
> Or simply acknowledge their feelings of frustration, anxiety, concern, etc.

In chapter 8, I advised you to use the word "but" between your two validating statements when addressing your inner critic; in that context, the word "but" reinforces the fact that your self-worth always takes precedence over your self-criticism. However, for mutual validation in interpersonal communication the word "but" can be incredibly invalidating, so you should generally try to avoid it. See how these examples show how "but" can impact the tone of a statement:

> "I love you, *but* sometimes you frustrate me."
>
> "You did a great job, *but* I think you could have improved a few things."
>
> "I see your point, *but* I disagree."

In these examples, the word "but" completely negates the first part of the statement, implying that whatever comes after the word "but" is more important. There's no point in validating someone if you're just going to undo it with the word "but." Here are some phrases you can use instead:

> "On my end . . ."
>
> "From my point of view . . ."
>
> "In my experience . . ."
>
> "What I prefer is . . ."
>
> Or even just a simple pause

Once you've validated the other person's perspective, it's time to validate your own. Simply state how you feel or what you think. Since you started by validating the other person, they now feel heard and understood. They know you're not simply trying to argue or prove them wrong. They're prepared to listen. Granted, it's not a guarantee that they will listen. Some people need to work on that skill. But at least you've done everything you can to minimize the odds of starting an argument.

Mutual validation can be especially helpful when you need to say no to someone. People generally don't like to hear the word "no," so when you have to communicate disagreement or decline a request, it's important that you do so thoughtfully. Using mutual validation acknowledges the other person's situation or feeling while also validating your own need to establish a boundary. This way, the other person can more easily understand and accept your reasoning, since they feel that you understand and acknowledge their point of view. Here's an example:

> "I'm really sorry to hear that you didn't get the job you wanted. I need to work on an important project that's due tomorrow, so I won't be available tonight to support you."

When saying no to someone, it's completely up to you if you want to express sorrow for it or not. Some self-compassion gurus assert that you should never express sorrow when you haven't done anything wrong. They argue that there's no need to apologize for saying no because you're not obligated to comply with a person's request. In their view, by apologizing for it you diminish your self-worth by accepting guilt for exercising your right to decline a request.

While I understand this perspective, I also think it overlooks alternative meanings of the word "sorry." "Sorry" can express an apology, but it can also communicate empathy and understanding (e.g., "I'm sorry that happened to you"). Did you notice how I just used mutual validation to make my point? If you feel a strong urge to say "sorry" after saying no to someone, just ask yourself why. If it feels like a genuine expression of compassion, there's probably no cause for concern. But if you're apologizing for something that isn't your responsibility, it's best to try to refrain.

Technique #4: Assertive Pause

Have you ever said something in the heat of the moment and regretted it later? Have you ever felt pressured to say yes to a request or answer a question you weren't comfortable with? These are the kinds of situations that call for an assertive pause.

Most situations aren't urgent, so the idea behind the assertive pause is that it's okay to take some time to think about how to respond. When you're new to assertiveness, it's easy to forget that. If you aren't careful, you may respond to a request or inflammatory statement without thinking it through . . . then regret it later.

Taking an assertive pause simply means buying yourself some time before you respond to a question or statement. You'll almost always respond more honestly and thoughtfully when you've had a chance to think first. Without the pressure for an immediate response, you can weigh pros and cons, determine how to articulate your feelings, or gather more information so you can respond in a way that's both genuine and kind. Here are a few assertive phrases you can use when you need time to respond:

> "You've given me a lot to think about, and I want to take some time before I give a final answer."
>
> "Please give me a few moments to collect my thoughts before I respond."
>
> "I don't want my emotions to influence my response, so I need to calm down before I say anything else."
>
> "I'm not sure what I'm thinking, but I'll let you know once I've had a chance to make sense of it all."

While an assertive pause advocates for discussion *later*, it also doesn't define what *later* means. *Later* could mean 10 minutes from now, tomorrow, or even next week. That's up to your discretion based on what you need and what's appropriate for the situation. It's easy to believe that you can't use an assertive pause in time-sensitive situations, but even pausing for a couple of minutes, or even seconds, can be an effective way to manage a stressful situation and ensure that you don't say anything you don't really mean. It can give you time to take a walk, a deep breath, or, if you're hangry, a bite to eat. An assertive pause is just a bid for time—as much of it as you need.

Technique #5: The Broken Record

This is my personal favorite assertiveness technique. I love it because it's beautifully simple, surprisingly effective, and can drastically reduce your anxiety about how others might respond to your assertiveness.

As its name implies, the broken-record technique simply involves repeating the same central message over and over (and over) until it's received. Maybe you only need to repeat your message twice. Maybe you need to repeat it 10 times. But no matter what, usually you only need to stick to one simple statement. As long as it's reasonable, you don't need to justify it. When it comes to establishing boundaries, expressing discomfort, or rejecting undue criticism, you don't need to be eloquent; you just need to be firm.

One of the main reasons assertiveness can be so scary is because you can never predict with certainty how the other person will respond. You can prepare what you think is a clear and reasonable statement but get caught off guard if the other person pushes back or questions you. While you can (and should) consider their response to determine whether to bend a little, you get to decide whether or not to engage. As long as your stance is reasonable, the broken-record technique is the perfect solution to pushback. When you assert yourself, unless you are factually incorrect or being disrespectful, whatever you have to say is valid and you don't need to defend it. When you try to defend yourself, you imply that your needs, preferences, or feelings are up for negotiation. They're not.

To use the broken-record technique, all you need to do is stick to one point and repeat it as many times as necessary. Preferably just one sentence, because the same sentence repeated over and over really makes a statement that you're remaining firm. You don't need to explain or justify yourself unless you consider it absolutely necessary for the sake of mutual understanding.

There's no need to answer questions once you've made your point, because your answers can serve as ammunition for the other person to use against you. They can (knowingly or unknowingly) discredit your statement by diverting your attention to some other issue. Here's an example:

Person 1: "I prefer not to have my picture taken."

Person 2: "Why not? It's just a picture."

Person 1: "Because I feel self-conscious about how I look today."

Person 2: "Don't worry, you look great!"

Person 1: "Thank you, but I just think that seeing myself in this picture is going to bring me down."

Person 2: "Oh, you're just being overly critical of yourself. It's fine. Now get in the picture."

Person 1: "How about I take the picture instead of being in it?"

Person 2: "No, you need to be part of the memory."

When the other person isn't taking no for an answer, it can feel like you have less leverage over your own preferences, or that they aren't even valid. In these situations, you need to communicate that your original point stands even if the other person disagrees with it. After you've received pushback, either repeat your original statement or choose a more standard statement to repeat. Here are some examples:

> "I've made my decision and I don't wish to discuss it further."
>
> "I am entitled to my own opinion."
>
> "This is what I've determined is best for myself."
>
> "It's a personal preference."

Even though you're repeating the same message, that doesn't mean you have to be rude, condescending, or aggressive in the process. You can include softening statements that help maintain politeness while also being firm. Here's an example:

> Person 1: "I prefer not to have my picture taken."
>
> Person 2: "Why not? It's just a picture."
>
> Person 1: "I know. I'd just rather not."
>
> Person 2: "Are you worried about how you look? I think you look great!"
>
> Person 1: "Thank you, but it's just a preference and I'd rather not."
>
> Person 2: "But you need to be part of the memory."
>
> Person 1: "I understand and I'm sorry, but I would just prefer not to have my picture taken."
>
> Person 2: "Okay, if you insist. Would you mind taking the picture then?"

When you repeat the same point over and over, eventually the other person will get your point. They'll recognize that there's no room for negotiation and thus no point in continuing to raise counter-arguments. Standing up for yourself can feel like such an intimidating process, but sometimes it really is as simple as being a broken record.

Having Difficult Conversations

You've just learned five basic assertiveness techniques. Knowing how to use them can help you navigate a range of communication issues, but just knowing how to deliver a few one-liners is far from a comprehensive understanding of assertiveness. All the assertiveness techniques you've learned so far have the same limitation: they're short and only prepare you for conflicts that can be resolved in a few minutes. Not every situation is that simple and straightforward. Sometimes we need to have long and detailed conversations, and making 50 consecutive "I" statements just won't cut it. So when a conflict or request warrants a long conversation, what do you do? I've got some tips for that.

Be Direct

A question I get asked a lot when I'm helping a client address a sensitive topic with a loved one is some variation of "How do I bring it up?" My answer is (sometimes frustratingly) simple: just say it. Almost always, the most direct approach to assertiveness is the most effective one. What we often forget about assertiveness is that it absolutely must be genuine. Any attempt at being sly or subtle probably won't go unnoticed. Most people can recognize when someone is beating around the bush. The best policy is usually just to say what you need to say. It can feel pretty vulnerable to do that, but if you're not vulnerable, you can't have an open and honest conversation about important topics. Just like getting into a cold swimming pool, it's best to take the plunge and adapt to the shock rather than draw it out.

My hope is that my blunt advice on how to communicate a difficult point alleviates some pressure to be eloquent. Assertiveness isn't reserved only for people who are good with words. It's a vulnerable human experience, and hiding behind perfectly phrased statements isn't going to make it any less vulnerable. Just say what you need to say (with respect and sensitivity, of course). Once it's on the table, you can do something with it. The next section will help you determine how to "just say it."

Make Your Purpose Known

Do you remember in high school English class how every paper you wrote had to have a thesis statement? I have to admit, I was incredibly annoyed by them at the time. It took me a while to realize that a thesis statement helps readers understand your main point and guides their thoughts as they read, ensuring they process the information accurately. It really makes digesting a piece of writing, particularly a complex and multifaceted work, easier to understand. It turns out, thesis statements are invaluable, not just for writing but for assertiveness too.

What's your point? What are you hoping to get from the conversation? Are you asking the other person to change? Do you need their help? Do you just want them to understand and empathize with your perspective? It's immensely helpful for the other person to know this upfront. It's also helpful for you, the communicator, to have determined the purpose beforehand. How can you have an effective conversation without knowing what your goal is? Take some time to reflect before you bring your thoughts to the other person. Once you've decided on your goal, identify the main points that support your overall thesis statement. The conversation will go so much better, because you can make sure you both start on the same page. For example, you can make statements such as:

> "I want to tell you about something that's been bothering me so that we can work on resolving it."
>
> "I feel misunderstood, and I just want to clue you in on how I'm feeling because it's important to me that you know."
>
> "I feel like we're not on the same page, so I want to communicate what I'm feeling, and then I want to hear from you."

Even if you're not entirely sure what your goal is, you can still articulate that. For example, you can say, "I'm not exactly sure what I'm hoping to get from this conversation, but I want a chance to communicate my perspective and maybe that will give us both some clarity." Remember, communication is about being vulnerable, not about always knowing exactly what to say. Even when your purpose isn't completely fleshed out, simply cluing the other person in on where you are in the process is immensely important and helps them listen more openly.

One Thing at a Time

Let's face it, sometimes feelings fester. Maybe something minorly upsetting happens and we brush it off, but that minor thing happens again and again, and now we've got weeks' worth of data to be upset about. Or maybe the urge to avoid a difficult conversation is just too strong to resist, and without any release, an explosion later on becomes inevitable. In either of those cases, it's tempting to unload on someone. They've made you upset and you need to really hand it to them. That's an aggressive approach, and it's usually not effective at all.

If you want to be good at assertiveness, you need to master the art of restraint. Focusing on just one issue makes the conversation a lot more manageable. As much as you may want to, resist unloading a laundry list of complaints onto the other person. That's a great way to derail a conversation. You may need to use a few different examples to back up your main point, but only give the information that's necessary for the other person to understand where you're coming from, then stop. It's okay if you leave out a few points of evidence, as long as the other person understands your overall message. Perseverating on an issue only serves as catharsis for you, not mutual understanding and problem-solving.

Avoid generalizations. Words like "always," "never," and "every" shouldn't come out of your mouth if you're trying to be assertive. The other person's guard will shoot up so fast they'll get whiplash, and they'll be more focused on finding exceptions to your statement than being receptive to the issue you're trying to bring to their attention. Instead, be as specific as you can about a particular example, and only provide further examples if needed or requested.

Tune In to Your Anxiety

In my experience, anxiety tends to be one of the most difficult-to-overcome barriers to assertiveness. That's because assertiveness can be so vulnerable, and most of us would rather avoid vulnerability. What if the other person misunderstands? What if they disagree? What if they get mad? Your anxiety could identify a million terrifying possibilities if you let it. And a lot of people let those possibilities stop them.

The truth is, a lot could go wrong when you have an assertive conversation with someone. But your anxiety can help you a lot here. An important component of clear and effective communication is anticipating potential stumbling blocks and proactively avoiding them. For example, if you have a friend who tends to jump to conclusions, make sure you clearly establish the conclusion you'd like them to reach (or refute the conclusion you don't want them to reach) right away so they have no opportunity to take the leap. If you have a boss with a temper, you can make a contingency plan in advance so you know how to respond if they start to get heated. Tuning in to anxiety gives you the opportunity to foresee things you don't want to happen, then take steps to reduce the odds that they do happen.

Not only is it helpful for you to lean into your own anxiety to form contingency plans, but it can also be extremely helpful to acknowledge any potential anxiety the other person may experience during the conversation. For example, "we need to talk" have to be the four most anxiety-provoking words ever strung together. When you hear those words, you don't listen out of openness but out of fear. Your brain scans for signs of danger rather than thoughtfully absorbing information. It's important that you ensure the other person feels at ease during the conversation; that way they'll truly be able to listen to you without being too reactive. Of course, you shouldn't lie and say it's not a big deal if it actually is. But likely in any situation, there's something you can say to defuse the situation ahead of time.

Earlier, I encouraged you to state your purpose—your thesis statement—at the start of the conversation. But I also encourage you to be clear about what your purpose is *not*. In fact, this might be more important than your thesis statement itself. It can help ensure the other person listens with openness rather than anticipation by eliminating all possible conclusions other than the correct one. For example, you can preface your conversation by saying, "I'm not mad at you," "I'm not trying to say you're a bad friend," "I don't want to make you feel bad," etc. Just make sure whatever you say is honest and doesn't inadvertently become shorthand for "we need to talk."

Before initiating an assertive conversation, make a list of "what-ifs," then formulate a plan in case any of those possibilities occur. For example, if the other person yells, take an assertive pause. If they don't agree with what you're saying or asking, make a contingency plan. Tuning in to your anxiety by making a concrete plan for any potential complications can counterintuitively ease your anxiety tremendously. It helps you approach the conversation with considerably more confidence because you feel prepared. Just remember, you can't possibly prepare for everything, so don't obsess over this part. Prepare to the best of your abilities and approach the conversation with confidence in your communication skills.

Take Notes

Are you overwhelmed? There's a lot to take in, and it might feel like you'll never remember to use all these guidelines in a conversation. If you're feeling this way, I have some good news for you: you don't need to remember any of this.

Assertiveness is an open book exam! Jot down your main point, some bullet points, and supporting examples, then refer to it during your assertive conversation. Don't worry, this won't affect your reputation. People are often worried about how they'll look if they refer to their notes during a conversation. If anything, I think it could earn you some brownie points. It shows that you're taking the conversation seriously and have given it some thought. You've done your homework and you're prepared. Personally, I've got a lot of respect for that. There should be no shame in pulling out a note you've written for yourself. In fact, you can take ownership, like in these examples:

> "This is an important topic and I want to make sure I hit all of my main points."

> "I want to prevent any misunderstanding so I took some notes to make sure my points are clear."

Just make sure your list of bullet points isn't too extensive. If the other person sees that you've practically prepared a slideshow presentation of your thoughts, they might feel attacked.

There's an element of assertiveness that taking notes affects directly: anxiety. It can be so calming to have a plan going into a scary and uncertain situation. Not to mention, anxiety tends to cloud our thoughts. Maybe you can articulate your thoughts clearly when you're imagining the conversation, but the minute you face the other person, you don't even know which way is up. Your notes are your friend in this situation. Even a clouded brain can comprehend pre-written notes.

A word of caution though: don't write a monologue. Remember, the goal is to be genuine. Reading aloud an essay you wrote for the other person is going to seem scripted . . . because it literally is! Instead, just make some bullet points. You'll remember how to elaborate on your points, even with your cloudy thoughts. You just don't want to forget what your main points are.

Treat Anger and Resentment as Yield Signs

You've heard the adage *If you don't have anything nice to say, don't say anything at all*. The truth is, when we're feeling angry, hurt, or resentful, we can come up with some pretty mean things to say that we might not necessarily say in times of inner peace. And unfortunately, assertive conversations are almost always needed most when feelings like these are high. When you're in that emotional state, see it as a sign that you aren't ready to be assertive just yet. Trying to practice assertiveness while angry is an almost guaranteed way to accidentally act aggressively. Name-calling, yelling, and interrupting might slip into a conversation when you approach it with a mindset that's flooded with negative emotions. You may as well consider the conversation derailed before it begins. If you're noticing that it feels difficult to approach a conversation with a moderate level of sensitivity, consider using an assertive pause to allow yourself time to calm down and clear your head before opening up about your feelings. You'll be a lot more rational, respectful, and open if you do.

The Breakdown

As much information as I just threw at you, there really are just a few guiding principles that tie them all together. You may have even noticed some of them along the way. If you want a more intuitive understanding about how to be assertive without having to memorize multiple scripts and outlines, then understanding common themes can give you everything you need to do it all effectively.

The overarching goal of any assertiveness technique is to simply minimize the probability that the other person will become defensive. You might have noticed that every technique covered in this appendix shares this goal. You can prevent defensiveness by incorporating the following principles into your communication:

- **Take ownership over your own feelings or perspective.** Your feelings are your own responsibility, even if they were caused by the actions of others. When you communicate from your perspective, it's really all about you. When that's the case, there's realistically nothing for the other person to defend. Just remember that you're speaking *your truth*, not *The Truth*. That means being open to the possibility that the other person doesn't see things the same way you do, or maybe there's a vital piece of information you're missing that could change the whole situation. Not to mention, your perspective doesn't have to be "right" to be valid or deserving of someone else's attention (as long as it isn't offensive or disrespectful). Just take ownership over how you feel. I promise, it's important enough.

- **Avoid inflammatory language.** As long as you avoid shame-based language and generalizations, you'll be fine.
- **Anticipate the other person's roadblocks to listening openly.** If you can anticipate how a person might react to what you have to say, you can plan accordingly. You can rework your language, be more specific, or just be clear about why you're having the conversation in the first place. Anticipation is an extremely important skill in communication, so you should leverage it whenever possible.

By applying these principles to your communication, not only will your communication be more effective, but you'll approach conversations more confidently. When you avoid possibilities for defensiveness, you minimize the unknown element of adverse reactions that could completely derail a conversation. You'll feel more confident that a conversation will go smoothly, and you'll experience less fear in approaching it.

Self-Compassion Exercise:
Practicing Assertiveness

Countless circumstances in life call for assertiveness: expressing your emotions, establishing boundaries, reaching mutual understanding, making a request, saying no, and so many more. There will be no shortage of opportunity for you to practice all the techniques you've learned so you can sharpen your assertiveness skills and build your confidence. But that doesn't mean you need to jump right in at every opportunity life gives you—especially if this is all new to you. To avoid feeling overwhelmed, it may be more manageable to approach assertiveness opportunities systematically.

When facing something challenging or uncomfortable, using a hierarchy approach is a good way to go. This involves identifying and isolating elements of the issue you want to face, then ranking them in terms of difficulty or discomfort. Addressing the easiest elements, and then over time working your way up to the most difficult, will help you toe the fine line between challenging and overwhelming. There's no growth without challenge, but you do yourself no favors by overloading yourself with challenges either.

When it comes to practicing assertiveness, there are numerous contexts, which all affect how intimidating the situation feels. Before you begin practicing your assertiveness skills, identify the best starting points. In the following tables indicate how difficult each of the following elements of assertiveness are to you. You can assign each factor a number (such as a difficulty level from 0 to 10, for example) or an ordinal designation (such as easy, moderate, or difficult). However you decide to approach the tables, make sure you're able to rank each factor in terms of its difficulty for you. If you come up with other elements that aren't represented in these tables, feel free to add them.

To download a free copy of this worksheet, visit rethinkyourself.info/worksheets or scan the QR code in the back of the book.

What	Difficulty
Making a simple request	
Asking for assistance (specify below if needed)	
» emotional support	
» tangible support (such as financial)	
» social support (such as advice and brainstorming)	
Communicating emotions	
Seeking mutual understanding	
Stating a preference	
Stating an opinion	
Asking for a promotion	
Communicating sexual preferences	
Saying no	
Addressing conflict	
Disagreeing	

Who	Difficulty
Parent(s) (specify parents individually if needed)	
People of the same gender as mine	
People of a different gender than mine	
Siblings	
Extended family	
Boss/Manager/Supervisor	
Coworkers/Colleagues/Classmates	
Teacher/Professor	
Religious authority figure	
Strangers	
Close friends	
Acquaintances	
Groups of three or more people	
People I find attractive	
People older than me	
People younger than me	
Authority figures	

When	Difficulty
I'm feeling angry	
I'm feeling disappointed	
I'm feeling sad	
I'm feeling guilty	
I'm feeling worried	
I'm feeling overwhelmed	
I'm feeling confused	
I'm feeling jealous	
I'm feeling disrespected	
I might look weak	

I'm tired	
I can't predict the person's response	
I think I might cry	
The other person is upset	
Others are around to observe	

Now you have a starting point. Use assertiveness in any context you currently consider at least moderately easy. As you're starting out, give yourself permission to defer assertiveness in the more difficult or uncomfortable contexts. You'll address those once you've built up more confidence. As time goes on and you feel like you've refined your skills a bit, start to identify opportunities for assertiveness that feel more challenging, and make it a point to take on those opportunities. Eventually you'll work all the way up to the most difficult contexts. The most important thing is that you proceed at your own pace.

You may proceed in any fashion you like. Assertiveness is highly dependent on circumstance and individual characteristics, so you'll have to be opportunistic. You usually can't proactively structure opportunities at will; they just tend to happen. Challenge yourself bit by bit, and eventually you'll see that what you used to view as challenging is now much easier.

Remember that assertiveness is an act of self-worth, and you have to acknowledge that for it to fully sink in. Each time you communicate with assertiveness, remind yourself that you did it because you're worth the respect, fairness, patience, or help that you request from others. Here are some examples of statements you can say to yourself to really drive the point home:

"I stood up for myself because I'm worthy of respect."

"That was a difficult conversation, but I'm worth the effort it took."

"I'm entitled to my preferences."

"I'm worthy of help."

If you want, use the spaces on the next page to record and evaluate your assertiveness techniques so that you continue to improve (but that's not required):

To download a free copy of this worksheet, visit rethinkyourself.info/worksheets or scan the QR code in the back of the book.

Situation (what, who, when):

_____

Perceived difficulty level: _____

Actual difficulty level: _____

Communication technique(s) used:

_____

How I can improve:

_____

Self-worth reflection:

_____

Situation (what, who, when):

_____

Perceived difficulty level: _____

Actual difficulty level: _____

Communication technique(s) used:

_____

How I can improve:

_____

Self-worth reflection:

_____

Endnotes

Chapter 1

[1] Nathaniel Branden. *The Six Pillars of Self-Esteem: The Definitive Work on Self-Esteem by the Leading Pioneer in the Field* (Bantam, 1995).

[2] Roland Zahn, Karen E. Lythe, Jennifer A. Gethin, Sophie Green, John F. William Deakin, Allan H. Young, and Jorge Moll. "The Role of Self-Blame and Worthlessness in the Psychopathology of Major Depressive Disorder." *Journal of Affective Disorders*, 186 (2015). https://doi.org/10.1016/j.jad.2015.08.001.

[3] M. Rutter. "Resilience in the Face of Adversity. Protective Factors and Resistance to Psychiatric Disorder." *The British Journal of Psychiatry: The Journal of Mental Science* 147 (1985). https://doi.org/10.1192/bjp.147.6.598; Kenichiro Ishizu. "Contingent Self-Worth Moderates the Relationship Between School Stressors and Psychological Stress Responses." *Journal of Adolescence* 56 (2017). https://doi.org/10.1016/j.adolescence.2017.02.008.

Chapter 3

[1] William E. Copeland, Dieter Wolke, Adrian Angold, and E. Jane Costello. "Adult Psychiatric Outcomes of Bullying and Being Bullied by Peers in Childhood and Adolescence." *JAMA Psychiatry* 70, no. 4 (2013). https://doi.org/10.1001/jamapsychiatry.2013.504.

[2] Morten Birkeland Nielsen, Tone Tangen, Thormod Idsoe, Stig Berge Matthiesen, and Nils Magerøy. "Post-Traumatic Stress Disorder as a Consequence of Bullying at Work and at School. A Literature Review and Meta-Analysis." *Aggression and Violent Behavior* 21 (2015). https://doi.org/10.1016/j.avb.2015.01.001.

[3] Mona O'Moore and C. Kirkham. "Self-Esteem and Its Relationship to Bullying Behaviour." *Aggressive Behavior* 27, no. 4 (2001). https://doi.org/10.1002/ab.1010; Sharon Callaghan and Stephen Joseph. "Self-Concept and Peer Victimization Among Schoolchildren." *Personality and Individual Differences* 18, no. 1 (1995). https://doi.org/10.1016/0191-8869(94)00127-E.

[4] Justin W. Patchin and Sameer Hinduja. "Cyberbullying and Self-Esteem." *The Journal of School Health* 80, no. 12 (2010). https://doi.org/10.1111/j.1746-1561.2010.00548.x.

[5] Michelle A. Harris, Andrea E. Gruenenfelder-Steiger, Emilio Ferrer, M. Brent Donnellan, Mathias Allemand, Helmut Fend, Rand D. Conger, and Kali H. Trzesniewski. "Do Parents Foster Self-Esteem? Testing the Prospective Impact of Parent Closeness on Adolescent Self-Esteem." *Child Development* 86, no. 4 (2015). https://doi.org/10.1111/cdev.12356.

[6] Joan Newman, Hamide Gozu, Shuyi Guan, Ji Eun Lee, Xian Li, and Yuriko Sasaki. "Relationship Between Maternal Parenting Style and High School Achievement and Self-Esteem in China, Turkey and U.S.A." *Journal of Comparative Family Studies* 46, no. 2 (2015). https://doi.org/10.3138/jcfs.46.2.265.

[7] Matthew H. Logan. "Stockholm Syndrome: Held Hostage by the One You Love." *Violence and Gender* 5, no. 2 (2018). https://doi.org/10.1089/vio.2017.0076.

[8] Claire Arene. "The Impact of Being in an Unhealthy Relationship." HealthyPlace. December 22, 2021. Accessed January 3, 2024. https://www.healthyplace.com/relationships/unhealthy-relationships/the-impact-of-being-in-an-unhealthy-relationship.

[9] Todd K. Shackelford. "Self-Esteem in Marriage." *Personality and Individual Differences* 30, no. 3 (2001). https://doi.org/10.1016/S0191-8869(00)00023-4.

[10] Sofia Fernandez and Mary Pritchard. "Relationships Between Self-Esteem, Media Influence and Drive for Thinness." *Eating Behaviors* 13, no. 4 (2012). https://doi.org/10.1016/j.eatbeh.2012.05.004; Gayle R. Bessenoff. "Can the Media Affect Us? Social Comparison, Self-Discrepancy, and the Thin Ideal." *Psychology of Women Quarterly* 30, no. 3 (2006). https://doi.org/10.1111/j.1471-6402.2006.00292.x.

[11] Wei Peng, Qian Huang, Bingjing Mao, Di Lun, Ekaterina Malova, Jazmyne V. Simmons, and Nick Carcioppolo. "When Guilt Works: A Comprehensive Meta-Analysis of Guilt Appeals." *Frontiers in Psychology* 14 (2023). https://doi.org/10.3389/fpsyg.2023.1201631.

[12] Erin A. Vogel, Jason P. Rose, Lindsay R. Roberts, and Katheryn Eckles. "Social Comparison, Social Media, and Self-Esteem." *Psychology of Popular Media Culture* 3, no. 4 (2014). https://doi.org/10.1037/ppm0000047; Dian A. de Vries and Rinaldo Kühne. "Facebook and Self-Perception: Individual Susceptibility to Negative Social Comparison on Facebook." Personality and Individual Differences, 86 (2015). https://doi.org/10.1016/j.paid.2015.05.029; Claire Midgley, Sabrina Thai, Penelope Lockwood, Chloe Kovacheff, and Elizabeth Page-Gould. "When Every Day Is a High School Reunion: Social Media Comparisons and Self-Esteem." *Journal of Personality and Social Psychology* 121, no. 2 (2021). https://doi.org/10.1037/pspi0000336; J. P. Gerber, Ladd Wheeler, and Jerry Suls. "A Social Comparison Theory Meta-Analysis 60+ Years On." *Psychological Bulletin* 144, no. 2 (2018). https://doi.org/10.1037/bul0000127.

[13] Hui-Tzu Grace Chou and Nicholas Edge. "'They Are Happier and Having Better Lives Than I Am': The Impact of Using Facebook on Perceptions of Others' Lives." *Cyberpsychology, Behavior, and Social Networking* 15, no. 2 (2012). https://doi.org/10.1089/cyber.2011.0324; de Vries and Kühne. "Facebook and Self-Perception."

[14] Claire Midgley, Sabrina Thai, Penelope Lockwood, Chloe Kovacheff, and Elizabeth Page-Gould. "When Every Day Is a High School Reunion: Social Media Comparisons and Self-Esteem." *Journal of Personality and Social Psychology* 121, no. 2 (2021). https://doi.org/10.1037/pspi0000336.

[15] Robert E. Wilson, Samuel D. Gosling, and Lindsay T. Graham. "A Review of Facebook Research in the Social Sciences." *Perspectives on Psychological Science* 7, no. 3 (2012). https://doi.org/10.1177/1745691612442904.

[16] Julie Ann McMullin and John Cairney. "Self-Esteem and the Intersection of Age, Class, and Gender." *Journal of Aging Studies* 18, no. 1 (2004). https://doi.org/10.1016/j.jaging.2003.09.006.

[17] Jessica J. Good and Diana T. Sanchez. "Doing Gender for Different Reasons: Why Gender Conformity Positively and Negatively Predicts Self-Esteem." *Psychology of Women Quarterly* 34, no. 2 (2010). https://doi.org/10.1111/j.1471-6402.2010.01562.x.

[18] Roberto L. Abreu, Samuel J. Skidmore, Koree S. Badio, G. Tyler Lefevor, Karina A. Gattamorta, and Ryan J. Watson. "Sexual Harassment, Sexual Assault, Violence, Self-Esteem, and the Role of LGBTQ-Specific Parental Support in a Sample of Latinx Sexual and Gender Minority Youth." *Journal of Adolescence* (2023). https://doi.org/10.1002/jad.12210.

[19] Femke van den Brink, Manja Vollmann, and Shane van Weelie. "Relationships Between Transgender Congruence, Gender Identity Rumination, and Self-Esteem in Transgender and Gender-Nonconforming Individuals." *Psychology of Sexual Orientation and Gender Diversity* 7, no. 2 (2020). https://doi.org/10.1037/sgd0000357.

[20] Kristie Seelman, Michael Woodford, and Z. Nicolazzo. "Victimization and Microaggressions Targeting LGBTQ College Students: Gender Identity as a Moderator of Psychological Distress." *SW Publications* 77 (2016). https://scholarworks.gsu.edu/ssw_facpub/77; Tse-Chuan Yang, I.-Chien Chen, Seung-Won Choi, and Aysenur Kurtulus. "Linking Perceived Discrimination During Adolescence to Health During Mid-Adulthood: Self-Esteem and Risk-Behavior Mechanisms." *Social Science & Medicine* 232 (1982). https://doi.org/10.1016/j.socscimed.2018.06.012; Jeffrey E. Stokes. "Social Integration, Perceived Discrimination, and Self-Esteem in Mid- and Later Life: Intersections with Age and Neuroticism." *Aging & Mental Health* 23, no. 6 (2019). https://doi.org/10.1080/13607863.2018.1450834.

[21] Derald Wing Sue. *Microaggressions in Everyday Life: Race, Gender, and Sexual Orientation* (John Wiley & Sons Inc, 2010).

[22] Kevin L. Nadal. "Gender Microaggressions: Implications for Mental Health." *Feminism and Women's Rights Worldwide* 2 (2010).

[23] Kevin L. Nadal, Yinglee Wong, Katie E. Griffin, Kristin Davidoff, and Julie Sriken. "The Adverse Impact of Racial Microaggressions on College Students' Self-Esteem." *Journal of College Student Development* 55, no. 5 (2014). https://doi.org/10.1353/csd.2014.0051; Seelman et al. "Victimization and Microaggressions."

[24] Laura Doering. "Was It Me or Was It Gender Discrimination? How Women Respond to Ambiguous Incidents at Work." Sociological Science 10, no. 8 (2023). http://dx.doi.org/10.15195/v10.a18

[25] "Mental Illness." National Institute of Mental Health (NIMH). Accessed January 3, 2024. https://www.nimh.nih.gov/health/statistics/mental-illness.

[26] Anne K. Risch, Astrid Buba, Uwe Birk, Nexhmedin Morina, Melanie C. Steffens, and Ulrich Stangier. "Implicit Self-Esteem in Recurrently Depressed Patients." *Journal of Behavior Therapy and Experimental Psychiatry* 41, no. 3 (2010). https://doi.org/10.1016/j.jbtep.2010.01.003; Julia Friederike Sowislo and Ulrich Orth. "Does Low Self-Esteem Predict Depression and Anxiety? A Meta-Analysis of Longitudinal Studies." *Psychological Bulletin* 139, no. 1 (2013). https://doi.org/10.1037/a0028931.

[27] Sang Kyoung Kahng and Carol Mowbray. "Factors Influencing Self-Esteem Among Individuals with Severe Mental Illness: Implications for Social Work." *Social Work Research* 28, no. 4 (2004).

[28] Azure Reid-Russell, Adam Bryant Miller, Dario Cvencek, Andrew N. Meltzoff, and Katie A. McLaughlin. "Lower Implicit Self-Esteem as a Pathway Linking Childhood Abuse to Depression and Suicidal Ideation." *Development and Psychopathology* 34, no. 4 (2022). https://doi.org/10.1017/S0954579420002217; Brent K. Morrow and Gwendolyn T. Sorell. "Factors Affecting Self-Esteem, Depression, and Negative Behaviors in Sexually Abused Female Adolescents." *Journal of Marriage and the Family* 51, no. 3 (1989). https://doi.org/10.2307/352167; Francisco Carrillo-Alvarez. "Associations Between Trauma History and Dimensions of Self-Concept in College Students." *Honors Scholar Theses* (2022). https://digitalcommons.lib.uconn.edu/srhonors_theses/891.

[29] Mike Startup, Lebogang Makgekgenene, and Rosemary Webster. "The Role of Self-Blame for Trauma as Assessed by the Posttraumatic Cognitions Inventory (PTCI): A Self-Protective Cognition?" *Behaviour Research and Therapy* 45, no. 2 (2007). https://doi.org/10.1016/j.brat.2006.02.003; Catrina Brown. "Women's Narratives of Trauma: (Re)Storying Uncertainty, Minimization and Self-Blame." *Narrative Works* 3, no. 1 (2019). https://doi.org/10.7202/1062052ar.

[30] Annie Maheux and Matthew Price. "The Indirect Effect of Social Support on Post-Trauma Psychopathology via Self-Compassion." *Personality and Individual Differences* 88 (2016). https://doi.org/10.1016/j.paid.2015.08.051; Morrow and Sorell. "Factors Affecting Self-Esteem."

[31] Anna Zeira. "Mental Health Challenges Related to Neoliberal Capitalism in the United States." *Community Mental Health Journal* 58, no. 2 (2022). https://doi.org/10.1007/s10597-021-00840-7; Tim Kasser, Steve Cohn, Allen D. Kanner, and Richard M. Ryan. "Some Costs of American Corporate Capitalism: A Psychological Exploration of Value and Goal Conflicts." *Psychological Inquiry* 18, no. 1 (2007). https://doi.org/10.1080/10478400701386579.

[32] Audrey M. W. Simons, Annemarie Koster, Daniëlle A. I. Groffen, and Hans Bosma. "Perceived Classism and Its Relation with Socioeconomic Status, Health, Health Behaviours and Perceived Inferiority: The Dutch Longitudinal Internet Studies for the Social Sciences (LISS) Panel." *International Journal of Public Health* 62, no. 4 (2017). https://doi.org/10.1007/s00038-016-0880-2; Lloyd Brandts, Hans Bosma, Audrey Simons, Danielle Groffen, and Van Den Marjan Akker. "The Socioeconomic Roots of Shame and Perceptions of Social Inadequacy." *MaRBLe* 2 (2014). https://doi.org/10.26481/marble.2014.v2.318; Jean M. Twenge and W. Keith Campbell. "Self-Esteem and Socioeconomic Status: A Meta-Analytic Review." *Personality and Social Psychology Review* 6, no. 1 (2002). https://doi.org/10.1207/S15327957PSPR0601_3.

[33] Quanlei Yu, Jianwen Chen, Qiuying Zhang, and Shenghua Jin. "Implicit and Explicit Self-Esteem: The Moderating Effect of Individualism." *Social Behavior and Personality* 43, no. 3 (2015). https://doi.org/10.2224/sbp.2015.43.3.519.

[34] Romin W. Tafarodi and William B. Swann Jr. "Self-Liking and Self-Competence as Dimensions of Global Self-Esteem: Initial Validation of a Measure." *Journal of Personality Assessment* 65, no. 2 (1995). https://doi.org/10.1207/s15327752jpa6502_8.

[35] Romin W. Tafarodi and William B. Swann Jr. "Individualism-Collectivism and Global Self-Esteem: Evidence for a Cultural Trade-Off." *Journal of Cross-Cultural Psychology* 27, no. 6 (1996). https://doi.org/10.1177/0022022196276001.

Chapter 4

[1] Lucia Martinčeková and Robert D. Enright. "The Effects of Self-Forgiveness and Shame-Proneness on Procrastination: Exploring the Mediating Role of Affect." *Current Psychology* 39, no. 2 (2020). https://doi.org/10.1007/s12144-018-9926-3; Ronda L. Fee and June P. Tangney. "Procrastination: A Means of Avoiding Shame or Guilt?" *Journal of Social Behavior & Personality* 15, no. 5 (2000).

[2] Nelson Cowan, Eryn J. Adams, Sabrina Bhangal, Mike Corcoran, Reed Decker, Ciera E. Dockter, Abby T. Eubank, et al. "Foundations of Arrogance: A Broad Survey and Framework for Research." *Review of General Psychology* 23, no. 4 (2019). https://doi.org/10.1177/1089268019877138; Eddie Brummelman, Sander Thomaes, and Constantine Sedikides. "Separating Narcissism from Self-Esteem." *Current Directions in Psychological Science* 25, no. 1 (2016). https://doi.org/10.1177/0963721415619737.

[3] Matthew McKay and Patrick Fanning. Self-Esteem: *A Proven Program of Cognitive Techniques for Assessing, Improving, and Maintaining Your Self-Esteem.* Fourth Edition (New Harbinger Publications, 2016).

Chapter 6

[1] Daniel C. Molden and E. Tory Higgins. "Motivated Thinking." In *The Cambridge Handbook of Thinking and Reasoning* (Cambridge University Press, 2005), 295–317; Uwe Peters. "What Is the Function of Confirmation Bias?" *Erkenntnis* 87, no. 3 (2022). https://doi.org/10.1007/s10670-020-00252-1.

[2] Brendan Nyhan and Jason Reifler. "Does Correcting Myths About the Flu Vaccine Work? An Experimental Evaluation of the Effects of Corrective Information." *Vaccine* 33, no. 3 (2015). https://doi.org/10.1016/j.vaccine.2014.11.017.

[3] Brendan Nyhan and Jason Reifler. "When Corrections Fail: The Persistence of Political Misperceptions." *Political Behavior* 32, no. 2 (2010). https://doi.org/10.1007/s11109-010-9112-2.

Chapter 7

[1] Brené Brown. *I Thought It Was Just Me (But It Isn't): Making the Journey from "What Will People Think" to "I Am Enough"* (Avery, 2007).

[2] Martinčeková and Enright. "The Effects of Self-Forgiveness"; Fee and Tangney. "Procrastination."

Chapter 12

[1] Jordi Quoidbach, June Gruber, Moïra Mikolajczak, Alexsandr Kogan, Ilios Kotsou, and Michael I. Norton. "Emodiversity and the Emotional Ecosystem." *Journal of Experimental Psychology: General* 143, no. 6 (2014). https://doi.org/10.1037/a0038025.

[2] Jonathan M. Adler and Hal E. Hershfield. "Mixed Emotional Experience Is Associated with and Precedes Improvements in Psychological Well-Being." *PLOS ONE* 7, no. 4 (2012). https://doi.org/10.1371/journal.pone.0035633; Hal E. Hershfield, Susanne Scheibe, Tamara L. Sims, and Laura L. Carstensen. "When Feeling Bad Can Be Good: Mixed Emotions Benefit Physical Health Across Adulthood." *Social Psychological and Personality Science* 4, no. 1 (2013). https://doi.org/10.1177/1948550612444616.

Works Cited

Abreu, Roberto L., Samuel J. Skidmore, Koree S. Badio, G. Tyler Lefevor, Karina A. Gattamorta, and Ryan J. Watson. "Sexual Harassment, Sexual Assault, Violence, Self-Esteem, and the Role of LGBTQ-Specific Parental Support in a Sample of Latinx Sexual and Gender Minority Youth." *Journal of Adolescence* (2023). https://doi.org/10.1002/jad.12210.

Adler, Jonathan M., and Hal E. Hershfield. "Mixed Emotional Experience Is Associated with and Precedes Improvements in Psychological Well-Being." *PLOS ONE* 7, no. 4 (2012). https://doi.org/10.1371/journal.pone.0035633.

Arene, Claire. "The Impact of Being in an Unhealthy Relationship." HealthyPlace. December 22, 2021. Accessed January 3, 2024. https://www.healthyplace.com/relationships/unhealthy-relationships/the-impact-of-being-in-an-unhealthy-relationship.

Bessenoff, Gayle R. "Can the Media Affect Us? Social Comparison, Self-Discrepancy, and the Thin Ideal." *Psychology of Women Quarterly* 30, no. 3 (2006): 239–51. https://doi.org/10.1111/j.1471-6402.2006.00292.x.

Branden, Nathaniel. *The Six Pillars of Self-Esteem: The Definitive Work on Self-Esteem by the Leading Pioneer in the Field* (Bantam, 1995).

Brandts, Lloyd, Hans Bosma, Audrey Simons, Danielle Groffen, and Van Den Marjan Akker. "The Socioeconomic Roots of Shame and Perceptions of Social Inadequacy." *MaRBLe* 2 (2014). https://doi.org/10.26481/marble.2014.v2.318.

Brown, Brené. *I Thought It Was Just Me (But It Isn't): Making the Journey from "What Will People Think" to "I Am Enough"* (Avery, 2007).

Brown, Catrina. "Women's Narratives of Trauma: (Re)Storying Uncertainty, Minimization and Self-Blame." *Narrative Works* 3, no. 1 (2019). https://doi.org/10.7202/1062052ar.

Brummelman, Eddie, Sander Thomaes, and Constantine Sedikides. "Separating Narcissism from Self-Esteem." *Current Directions in Psychological Science* 25, no. 1 (2016): 8–13. https://doi.org/10.1177/0963721415619737.

Butler, Stephen. "The Impact of Advanced Capitalism on Well-Being: An Evidence-Informed Model." *Human Arenas* 2, no. 2 (2019): 200–27. https://doi.org/10.1007/s42087-018-0034-6.

Callaghan, Sharon, and Stephen Joseph. "Self-Concept and Peer Victimization Among School-children." *Personality and Individual Differences* 18, no. 1 (1995): 161–63. https://doi.org/10.1016/0191-8869(94)00127-E.

Carrillo-Alvarez, Francisco. "Associations Between Trauma History and Dimensions of Self-Concept in College Students." *Honors Scholar Theses* (2022). https://digitalcommons.lib.uconn.edu/srhonors_theses/891.

Chou, Hui-Tzu Grace, and Nicholas Edge. "'They Are Happier and Having Better Lives Than I Am': The Impact of Using Facebook on Perceptions of Others' Lives." *Cyberpsychology, Behavior, and Social Networking* 15, no. 2 (2012): 117–21. https://doi.org/10.1089/cyber.2011.0324.

Copeland, William E., Dieter Wolke, Adrian Angold, and E. Jane Costello. "Adult Psychiatric Outcomes of Bullying and Being Bullied by Peers in Childhood and Adolescence." *JAMA Psychiatry* 70, no. 4 (2013): 419–26. https://doi.org/10.1001/jamapsychiatry.2013.504.

Cowan, Nelson, Eryn J. Adams, Sabrina Bhangal, Mike Corcoran, Reed Decker, Ciera E. Dockter, Abby T. Eubank, et al. "Foundations of Arrogance: A Broad Survey and Framework for Research." *Review of General Psychology* 23, no. 4 (2019): 425–43. https://doi.org/10.1177/1089268019877138.

de Vries, Dian A., and Rinaldo Kühne. "Facebook and Self-Perception: Individual Susceptibility to Negative Social Comparison on Facebook." *Personality and Individual Differences,* 86 (2015): 217–21. https://doi.org/10.1016/j.paid.2015.05.029.

Doering, Laura. "'Was It Me or Was It Gender Discrimination?' How Women Respond to Ambiguous Incidents at Work." *Sociological Science* 10, no. 8 (2023): 501–33. http://dx.doi.org/10.15195/v10.a18

Fee, Ronda L., and June P. Tangney. "Procrastination: A Means of Avoiding Shame or Guilt?" *Journal of Social Behavior & Personality* 15, no. 5 (2000): 167–84.

Fernandez, Sofia, and Mary Pritchard. "Relationships Between Self-Esteem, Media Influence and Drive for Thinness." *Eating Behaviors* 13, no. 4 (2012): 321–25. https://doi.org/10.1016/j.eatbeh.2012.05.004.

Gerber, J. P., Ladd Wheeler, and Jerry Suls. "A Social Comparison Theory Meta-Analysis 60+ Years On." *Psychological Bulletin* 144, no. 2 (2018): 177–97. https://doi.org/10.1037/bul0000127.

Good, Jessica J., and Diana T. Sanchez. "Doing Gender for Different Reasons: Why Gender Conformity Positively and Negatively Predicts Self-Esteem." *Psychology of Women Quarterly* 34, no. 2 (2010): 203–14. https://doi.org/10.1111/j.1471-6402.2010.01562.x.

Harris, Michelle A., Andrea E. Gruenenfelder-Steiger, Emilio Ferrer, M. Brent Donnellan, Mathias Allemand, Helmut Fend, Rand D. Conger, and Kali H. Trzesniewski. "Do Parents Foster Self-Esteem? Testing the Prospective Impact of Parent Closeness on Adolescent Self-Esteem." *Child Development* 86, no. 4 (2015): 995–1013. https://doi.org/10.1111/cdev.12356.

Hershfield, Hal E., Susanne Scheibe, Tamara L. Sims, and Laura L. Carstensen. "When Feeling Bad Can Be Good: Mixed Emotions Benefit Physical Health Across Adulthood." *Social Psychological and Personality Science* 4, no. 1 (2013): 54–61. https://doi.org/10.1177/1948550612444616.

Ishizu, Kenichiro. "Contingent Self-Worth Moderates the Relationship Between School Stressors and Psychological Stress Responses." *Journal of Adolescence* 56 (2017): 113–17. https://doi.org/10.1016/j.adolescence.2017.02.008.

Kahng, Sang Kyoung, and Carol Mowbray. "Factors Influencing Self-Esteem Among Individuals with Severe Mental Illness: Implications for Social Work." *Social Work Research* 28, no. 4 (2004): 225–36.

Kasser, Tim, Steve Cohn, Allen D. Kanner, and Richard M. Ryan. "Some Costs of American Corporate Capitalism: A Psychological Exploration of Value and Goal Conflicts." *Psychological Inquiry* 18, no. 1 (2007): 1–22. https://doi.org/10.1080/10478400701386579.

Logan, Matthew H. "Stockholm Syndrome: Held Hostage by the One You Love." *Violence and Gender* 5, no. 2 (2018): 67–69. https://doi.org/10.1089/vio.2017.0076.

Maheux, Annie, and Matthew Price. "The Indirect Effect of Social Support on Post-Trauma Psychopathology via Self-Compassion." *Personality and Individual Differences* 88 (2016): 102–7. https://doi.org/10.1016/j.paid.2015.08.051.

Martinčeková, Lucia, and Robert D. Enright. "The Effects of Self-Forgiveness and Shame-Proneness on Procrastination: Exploring the Mediating Role of Affect." *Current Psychology* 39, no. 2 (2020): 428–37. https://doi.org/10.1007/s12144-018-9926-3.

McKay, Matthew and Patrick Fanning. *Self-Esteem: A Proven Program of Cognitive Techniques for Assessing, Improving, and Maintaining Your Self-Esteem.* Fourth Edition (New Harbinger Publications, 2016).

McMullin, Julie Ann, and John Cairney. "Self-Esteem and the Intersection of Age, Class, and Gender." *Journal of Aging Studies* 18, no. 1 (2004): 75–90. https://doi.org/10.1016/j.jaging.2003.09.006.

"Mental Illness." National Institute of Mental Health (NIMH). Accessed January 3, 2024. https://www.nimh.nih.gov/health/statistics/mental-illness.

Midgley, Claire, Sabrina Thai, Penelope Lockwood, Chloe Kovacheff, and Elizabeth Page-Gould. "When Every Day Is a High School Reunion: Social Media Comparisons and Self-Esteem." *Journal of Personality and Social Psychology* 121, no. 2 (2021): 285–307. https://doi.org/10.1037/pspi0000336.

Molden, Daniel C., and E. Tory Higgins. "Motivated Thinking." In *The Cambridge Handbook of Thinking and Reasoning*, (Cambridge University Press, 2005), 295–317.

Morrow, K. Brent, and Gwendolyn T. Sorell. "Factors Affecting Self-Esteem, Depression, and Negative Behaviors in Sexually Abused Female Adolescents." *Journal of Marriage and the Family* 51, no. 3 (1989): 677–86. https://doi.org/10.2307/352167.

Nadal, Kevin L. "Gender Microaggressions: Implications for Mental Health." *Feminism and Women's Rights Worldwide* 2 (2010): 155–75.

Nadal, Kevin L., Yinglee Wong, Katie E. Griffin, Kristin Davidoff, and Julie Sriken. "The Adverse Impact of Racial Microaggressions on College Students' Self-Esteem." *Journal of College Student Development* 55, no. 5 (2014): 461–74. https://doi.org/10.1353/csd.2014.0051.

Newman, Joan, Hamide Gozu, Shuyi Guan, Ji Eun Lee, Xian Li, and Yuriko Sasaki. "Relationship Between Maternal Parenting Style and High School Achievement and Self–Esteem in China, Turkey and U.S.A." *Journal of Comparative Family Studies* 46, no. 2 (2015): 265–88. https://doi.org/10.3138/jcfs.46.2.265.

Nielsen, Morten Birkeland, Tone Tangen, Thormod Idsoe, Stig Berge Matthiesen, and Nils Magerøy. "Post-Traumatic Stress Disorder as a Consequence of Bullying at Work and at School. A Literature Review and Meta-Analysis." *Aggression and Violent Behavior* 21 (2015): 17–24. https://doi.org/10.1016/j.avb.2015.01.001.

Nyhan, Brendan, and Jason Reifler. "Does Correcting Myths About the Flu Vaccine Work? An Experimental Evaluation of the Effects of Corrective Information." *Vaccine* 33, no. 3 (2015): 459–64. https://doi.org/10.1016/j.vaccine.2014.11.017.

Nyhan, Brendan, and Jason Reifler. "When Corrections Fail: The Persistence of Political Misperceptions." *Political Behavior* 32, no. 2 (2010): 303–30. https://doi.org/10.1007/s11109-010-9112-2.

O'Moore, Mona and C. Kirkham. "Self-Esteem and Its Relationship to Bullying Behaviour." *Aggressive Behavior* 27, no. 4 (2001): 269–83. https://doi.org/10.1002/ab.1010.

Patchin, Justin W., and Sameer Hinduja. "Cyberbullying and Self-Esteem." *The Journal of School Health* 80, no. 12 (2010): 614–21. https://doi.org/10.1111/j.1746-1561.2010.00548.x.

Peng, Wei, Qian Huang, Bingjing Mao, Di Lun, Ekaterina Malova, Jazmyne V. Simmons, and Nick Carcioppolo. "When Guilt Works: A Comprehensive Meta-Analysis of Guilt Appeals." *Frontiers in Psychology* 14 (2023). https://doi.org/10.3389/fpsyg.2023.1201631.

Peters, Uwe. "What Is the Function of Confirmation Bias?" *Erkenntnis* 87, no. 3 (2022): 1351–76. https://doi.org/10.1007/s10670-020-00252-1.

Quoidbach, Jordi, June Gruber, Moïra Mikolajczak, Alexsandr Kogan, Ilios Kotsou, and Michael I. Norton. "Emodiversity and the Emotional Ecosystem." *Journal of Experimental Psychology: General* 143, no. 6 (2014): 2057–66. https://doi.org/10.1037/a0038025.

Reid-Russell, Azure, Adam Bryant Miller, Dario Cvencek, Andrew N. Meltzoff, and Katie A. McLaughlin. "Lower Implicit Self-Esteem as a Pathway Linking Childhood Abuse to Depression and Suicidal Ideation." *Development and Psychopathology* 34, no. 4 (2022): 1272–86. https://doi.org/10.1017/S0954579420002217.

Risch, Anne K., Astrid Buba, Uwe Birk, Nexhmedin Morina, Melanie C. Steffens, and Ulrich Stangier. "Implicit Self-Esteem in Recurrently Depressed Patients." *Journal of Behavior Therapy and Experimental Psychiatry* 41, no. 3 (2010): 199–206. https://doi.org/10.1016/j.jbtep.2010.01.003.

Rutter, M. "Resilience in the Face of Adversity. Protective Factors and Resistance to Psychiatric Disorder." *The British Journal of Psychiatry: The Journal of Mental Science* 147 (1985): 598–611. https://doi.org/10.1192/bjp.147.6.598.

Seelman, Kristie, Michael Woodford, and Z. Nicolazzo. "Victimization and Microaggressions Targeting LGBTQ College Students: Gender Identity as a Moderator of Psychological Distress." *SW Publications* 77 (2016). https://scholarworks.gsu.edu/ssw_facpub/77.

Shackelford, Todd K. "Self-Esteem in Marriage." *Personality and Individual Differences* 30, no. 3 (2001): 371–90. https://doi.org/10.1016/S0191-8869(00)00023-4.

Simons, Audrey M. W., Annemarie Koster, Daniëlle A. I. Groffen, and Hans Bosma. "Perceived Classism and Its Relation with Socioeconomic Status, Health, Health Behaviours and Perceived Inferiority: The Dutch Longitudinal Internet Studies for the Social Sciences (LISS) Panel." *International Journal of Public Health* 62, no. 4 (2017): 433–40. https://doi.org/10.1007/s00038-016-0880-2.

Sowislo, Julia Friederike, and Ulrich Orth. "Does Low Self-Esteem Predict Depression and Anxiety? A Meta-Analysis of Longitudinal Studies." *Psychological Bulletin* 139, no. 1 (2013): 213–40. https://doi.org/10.1037/a0028931.

Startup, Mike, Lebogang Makgekgenene, and Rosemary Webster. "The Role of Self-Blame for Trauma as Assessed by the Posttraumatic Cognitions Inventory (PTCI): A Self-Protective Cognition?" *Behaviour Research and Therapy* 45, no. 2 (2007): 395–403. https://doi.org/10.1016/j.brat.2006.02.003.

Stokes, Jeffrey E. "Social Integration, Perceived Discrimination, and Self-Esteem in Mid- and Later Life: Intersections with Age and Neuroticism." *Aging & Mental Health* 23, no. 6 (2019): 727–35. https://doi.org/10.1080/13607863.2018.1450834.

Sue, Derald Wing. *Microaggressions in Everyday Life: Race, Gender, and Sexual Orientation* (John Wiley & Sons Inc, 2010).

Tafarodi, Romin W., and William B. Swann Jr. "Self-Liking and Self-Competence as Dimensions of Global Self-Esteem: Initial Validation of a Measure." *Journal of Personality Assessment* 65, no. 2 (1995): 322–42. https://doi.org/10.1207/s15327752jpa6502_8.

Tafarodi, Romin W., and William B. Swann Jr. "Individualism-Collectivism and Global Self-Esteem: Evidence for a Cultural Trade-Off." *Journal of Cross-Cultural Psychology* 27, no. 6 (1996): 651–72. https://doi.org/10.1177/0022022196276001.

Twenge, Jean M., and W. Keith Campbell. "Self-Esteem and Socioeconomic Status: A Meta-Analytic Review." *Personality and Social Psychology Review* 6, no. 1 (2002): 59–71. https://doi.org/10.1207/S15327957PSPR0601_3.

van den Brink, Femke, Manja Vollmann, and Shane van Weelie. "Relationships Between Trans-gender Congruence, Gender Identity Rumination, and Self-Esteem in Transgender and Gender-Nonconforming Individuals." *Psychology of Sexual Orientation and Gender Diversity* 7, no. 2 (2020): 230–35. https://doi.org/10.1037/sgd0000357.

Vogel, Erin A., Jason P. Rose, Lindsay R. Roberts, and Katheryn Eckles. "Social Comparison, Social Media, and Self-Esteem." *Psychology of Popular Media Culture* 3, no. 4 (2014): 206–22. https://doi.org/10.1037/ppm0000047.

Wilson, Robert E., Samuel D. Gosling, and Lindsay T. Graham. "A Review of Facebook Research in the Social Sciences." *Perspectives on Psychological Science* 7, no. 3 (2012): 203–20. https://doi.org/10.1177/1745691612442904.

Yang, Tse-Chuan, I.-Chien Chen, Seung-Won Choi, and Aysenur Kurtulus. "Linking Perceived Dis-crimination During Adolescence to Health During Mid-Adulthood: Self-Esteem and Risk-Be-havior Mechanisms." *Social Science & Medicine* 232 (1982), 434–43. https://doi.org/10.1016/j.socscimed.2018.06.012.

Yu, Quanlei, Jianwen Chen, Qiuying Zhang, and Shenghua Jin. "Implicit and Explicit Self-Esteem: The Moderating Effect of Individualism." *Social Behavior and Personality* 43, no. 3 (2015): 519–28. https://doi.org/10.2224/sbp.2015.43.3.519.

Zahn, Roland, Karen E. Lythe, Jennifer A. Gethin, Sophie Green, John F. William Deakin, Allan H. Young, and Jorge Moll. "The Role of Self-Blame and Worthlessness in the Psycho-pathology of Major Depressive Disorder." *Journal of Affective Disorders* 186 (2015): 337–41. https://doi.org/10.1016/j.jad.2015.08.001.

Zeira, Anna. "Mental Health Challenges Related to Neoliberal Capitalism in the United States." *Community Mental Health Journal* 58, no. 2 (2022): 205–12. https://doi.org/10.1007/s10597-021-00840-7.

About the Author

Zach Leezer is the founder of Unbroken Therapy in Chicago, Illinois where he specializes in treating low self-esteem, anxiety, body image, and more. He earned his Bachelor's Degree in Sociology from Bradley University and his Master of Social Work from the University of Illinois at Chicago.

Zach started his career providing mental health services to individuals involved in the criminal justice system, and eventually transitioned to an outpatient therapy practice. His initial passion for helping those convicted of crimes is what incidentally sparked his passion for self-esteem. He believes that everyone has something to bring to the table, and everyone has innate value, regardless of their mistakes.

Zach takes an action-orientated and grounded approach to therapy. He enjoys working with inquisitive and introspective clients. He incorporates the sociological perspective into his work as a therapist and his writing because social forces are invisible yet powerful influences on our thoughts, behaviors, and even our self-esteem.

When Zach isn't working, he enjoys baking, watching horror movies, hiking, and cuddling with his cat.

To download free worksheets from this book, visit rethinkyourself.info/worksheets or scan this QR code.

www.ingramcontent.com/pod-product-compliance
Lightning Source LLC
Chambersburg PA
CBHW061734120626
46550CB00005B/1794